D0753442

Cracking
THE
GOLDEN STATE
EXAMINATION

1st Year Algebra

The Princeton Review

Cracking

THE GOLDEN STATE EXAMINATION

1st Year Algebra

by Rick Sliter

Random House, Inc.
New York
www.randomhouse.com/princetonreview

The independent Education Consultants Association recognizes The Princeton Review as a valuable resource for high school and college students applying to college and graduate schools.

Princeton Review, L.L.C.
2315 Broadway
New York, NY 10024

E-mail: comments@review.com

Copyright © 2000 by Princeton Review Publishing, L.L.C.

All rights reserved under International and Pan-American Copyright Conventions.

Published in the United States by Random House, Inc., New York, and simultaneously in Canada by Random House of Canada, Limited, Toronto.

ISBN 0-375-75352-4

Editor: Rachel Warren
Production Editor: Julieanna Lambert
Production Coordinator: Stephanie Martin

Manufactured in the United States of America on partially recycled paper.

9 8 7 6 5 4 3 2 1

Acknowledgments

I would like to thank the following people for their suggestions and enthusiasm in helping me create this book: Jennifer Abell, Brett Baird, Shon Bayer, Michael Beltramo, Michael Bergman, Ahrash Bissell, Sterling Bryson, Martin Butterick, Oliver Butterick, Paula-Ann Cabading, Kristen Carosielli, Karin Cooke, Julie and Mike Daniels, Rob Dougherty, Dr. Chris Dvorak, Kathleen Farrell, Ben Goldhammer, Melissa Hagan, Paul Kanarek, Chris Kennedy, Daniel Konisky, Lisa Lepson, Jeff Lewis, Ana Marcos, Leny Marcus-Riebli, Adam Miller, David Moore, Tom Purcell, Frank Riebli, Amy L. Robinson, Joel Rubin, Erik Sincoff, Dr. Peter Simpson, Judy Sliter, Zinnia Su, Fiona Tam, Reed Talada, Carin Teitelbaum, Randy Tennant, Karen Warren, Brant Wellman, and Clint Woods.

For production and editing help, thanks to Lesly Atlas, Laurie Barnett, and Rachel Warren. Special thanks to Gretchen Feder for all of her patience, assistance, and suggestions throughout the book.

Finally, to all those students and teachers who have purchased this book, I acknowledge you in your efforts to reach the highest levels of academia.

Contents

PART I 1

  1 The Mystery Exam: About the Golden State Examinations 3

  2 Structure and Strategies 11

PART II 19

  3 The Basics of Algebra 21

  4 Algebraic Equations 45

  5 Factoring Polynomials 69

  6 Graphing 95

  7 Geometry 113

  8 Special Topics 123

PART III 147

  9 The Princeton Review Algebra GSE Practice Test I 149

    Answers and Explanations 163

  10 The Princeton Review Algebra GSE Practice Test II 183

    Answers and Explanations 197

  11 The Princeton Review Algebra GSE Practice Test III 217

    Answers and Explanations 231

  12 The Princeton Review Algebra GSE Practice Test IV 251

    Answers and Explanations 265

ABOUT THE AUTHOR 283

Part 1

THE MYSTERY EXAM: ABOUT THE GOLDEN STATE EXAMINATIONS

WHAT ARE THE GOLDEN STATE EXAMS?

The Golden State Examinations (GSEs) were established by the State of California Board of Education in 1983 (so your parents never took them—that's why they have probably never heard of them and may not understand how important they are). The tests are designed to offer a rigorous examination in key academic subjects to students in grades 7 to 12. Students who pass have a variety of advantages over those who don't—including the fact that their school transcripts will be more attractive to college and admissions boards.

The GSE program has grown in the last few years, both in the number of different exams offered and the number of students who take at least one GSE. During the 1999–2000 academic year, thirteen different GSE exams will be administered, and California students will complete more than one million examinations. In 1998, more than 2,100 graduates earned the Golden State Seal Merit Diploma, which recognizes students who have "mastered their high school curriculum" (see below for more information on the Merit Diploma).

You probably purchased this book because a teacher recommended it or because you were told to get ready to take a GSE. Congratulations! This is the most thorough, most complete guide you can own to prepare for the GSEs. Our goal is simple—to get you ready for the Golden State Examination in Algebra.

WE'RE HERE TO HELP

Like we said earlier, the GSEs are a mystery to students. There aren't even any official practice tests that you can study. We're here to change all that. Our research and development teams have spent countless hours to ensure that this guide tells you everything you need to know to ace the GSEs. All of the information that is released about the GSEs is in this book. We've also spoken to students and teachers about their experiences with these tests and designed our content review around their feedback. In short, we have the inside scoop on the GSEs, and we're going to share it with you.

What's So Special About This Book?

GSEs test subject knowledge, as well as the application of that knowledge. The goal of this book is twofold. First, we want to help you remember or relearn some of the subject material that's covered in the exam. Second, we want you to become familiar with the structure of the GSE so that you'll know exactly what to do on test day.

We at The Princeton Review aren't big fans of standardized tests, and we understand the stress and challenge that a GSE presents. But with our techniques and some work on your part, you should be able to do well on these tests. There's just one more thing you might be wondering—why *should* I take the GSEs?

WHY SHOULD YOU TAKE THE GOLDEN STATE EXAMINATIONS?

There are many reasons why you should spend time and energy getting ready for the GSEs. They include:

- **Qualification for a Golden State Seal Merit Diploma**

  The Golden State Seal Merit Diploma is one of—if not *the*—highest academic awards given by the State of California. In the pages that follow, we will detail exactly how you can qualify for a Merit Diploma.

- **Recognition on Your Transcript**

  If you perform well on a GSE, you will receive recognition on your high school transcript. We'll tell you later how the scoring system and award processes work.

- **College Admissions Committees Will Love You!**

  A strong performance on the GSEs will make you look great to colleges and universities. Academic awards will demonstrate to schools that you can excel in an academic environment.

- **They Are Risk Free!**

  First, there is absolutely no fee to take a GSE, so you won't need to worry about spending money on these tests. Second, there is absolutely no penalty if you do not perform well on a GSE. A score that does not give you an award will not appear on your transcript. In fact, only you will know if you did *not* pass a GSE. Translation—you've got nothing to lose, and a ton to gain!

- **All the Things Your Teacher Would Say**

  There are academic benefits to passing the tests as well. If you asked your teacher, "Why should I take these exams?" your teacher would probably tell you that, in addition to all the benefits listed above, "These tests provide a great opportunity for you to demonstrate what you have learned throughout high school, with the possibility of receiving numerous awards and titles for strong academic performance. The Golden State Examinations are an academic challenge that can enrich your high school experience."

Although we'll be a little less formal in the way we say it, we agree with the teacher's advice. The GSEs are your chance to show off what you know. You should receive recognition for all your hard work, and you should have every tool in your hand to *ensure* that you do well.

HOW ARE STUDENTS RECOGNIZED FOR THEIR PERFORMANCE?

If you score within the highest levels on any one Golden State Examination, you will receive one of three awards: high honors, honors, or recognition. Say you take three GSEs, one in history, one in biology, and one in written composition. And say (because you used The Princeton Review test-prep books), you are among the lucky one-third of all students who pass the GSEs and earn the awards listed below:

Test	Award
Written Composition	High Honors
History	Honors
Biology	Recognition

See how it works? These awards are formally called Academic Excellence Awards. This means that students who receive one of these three awards will receive an Academic Excellence Award from the State of California. This will be recorded on your high school transcript, and you'll receive a gold insignia on your diploma if you get a score of high honors or honors. Now, what exactly do these mean?

- **High Honors:** This is the most prestigious award given to students on the GSE in Algebra. It will be given to approximately the top 10 percent of students. If you receive "high honors" on the GSE in Algebra, you will receive a special gold seal on your high school diploma, and your award will be placed on your permanent transcript. Further, you can use this result as part of the requirements necessary for pursuing the ultimate award, the Golden State Seal Merit Diploma.

- **Honors:** This is the second most prestigious award given to students on the GSE in Algebra. It will be given to approximately 12 percent of the students that take the exam (students who score in the 78th to 90th percentile). If you receive "honors" on the GSE Algebra, you will receive the same rewards as students who achieved a score of "high honors" (so, read above to see what you get).

- **Recognition:** This is the final type of Academic Excellence award given to students on the GSE in Algebra. It will be given to approximately 15 percent of the students that take the exam (students who score in the 66th to 78th percentile). If you receive an award of "recognition" on the GSE Algebra, you will receive notification of this achievement on your high school transcript. Further, you can use this result as part of the requirements necessary for pursuing the ultimate award, the Golden State Seal Merit Diploma.

Any one of these awards can be very helpful in signaling high achievement to colleges, universities, and employers. Golden State Scholars are also eligible for a Golden State Seal Merit Diploma.

What is the Golden State Seal Merit Diploma?

In July of 1996, the State of California developed a Golden State Seal Merit Diploma program to recognize high school graduates who demonstrated high performance in several different academic areas. The Golden State Seal Merit Diploma is the most prestigious award you can receive through the GSEs. In 1997, the first year in which the Golden State Seal Merit Diploma was issued, more than 1,300 high school seniors received the award. This number jumped to more than 2,100 in 1998 and will continue to increase as more students take the GSEs.

In order to receive the Merit Diploma, students must receive high honors, honors, or recognition designations on *six* Golden State Examinations. The specific tests and requirements are described below.

Which Six Exams Do You Need to Pass to Get the Merit Diploma?

You do not need to apply to receive a Golden State Seal Merit Diploma. You just need to complete four required examinations, plus two elective exams, and receive at least recognition for them. School districts track the performance of each student and submit the information to the California Department of Education.

The four exams that students must pass are:

1. English (Written Composition or Reading and Literature)

2. U.S. History

3. Mathematics (Algebra, Geometry, or High School Mathematics)

4. Science (Biology, Chemistry, Physics, or Coordinated Science)

In addition to the four required exams, you will take two other GSEs, selected from the following: Economics, Spanish Language, or Government and Civics. You may also complete an *additional* science, mathematics, or English exam as one of your electives. For example, let's say you complete both the Algebra and Geometry examinations. In this case, one of them will be counted as the *required* mathematics exam and the other as an elective.

WHAT MATERIAL IS COVERED ON THE GSE?

The Golden State Examinations are developed by a committee of teachers, university professors, and other education specialists. Each examination is designed and tested so that the content reflects the state standards for each subject. In general, you should expect that the information tested on a GSE will be similar to what you've been tested on during the academic year. The style and format of the GSE may be different, but the material should be just like the stuff you studied in class. Unlike many other high school examinations, the GSEs are not designed to trick or trap you. In Chapter 2, we'll discuss the specific format, structure, and scoring of the GSE in Algebra.

> Remember that only about one-third of all test takers is honored for their performance on the Golden State Examination. Translation: Two-thirds don't pass and receive no recognition! These tests aren't a shoo-in; you need to know the material and be familiar with the structure to pass. This book is your key.

SO, HERE'S THE DEAL

Below are all the frequently asked questions about the administration of the GSEs. If there's anything we don't cover or if you're still confused, ask your guidance counselor or teacher.

How are GSE Exams Scored?

Every GSE has specific scoring criteria based on its format, structure, and level of difficulty. See Chapter 2 (page 11) for more specific information about how the GSE in Algebra is scored.

As we mentioned, there is no penalty whatsoever for poor performance on a GSE. If you fail to receive one of the honors designations, there will be no mention of it on your academic transcript. Further, students who do not receive an honors designation on one GSE should still be encouraged to take additional GSEs. Each test is scored independently—performance on one GSE will have no impact on the scoring of any other GSE.

When Will I Receive My GSE Results?

Results from the Golden State Examinations are first sent to your school district. If you take a winter examination, you should expect to hear about your results in May. If you take a spring examination, you should expect to hear about your results once you return to school in the fall.

If you have any questions regarding your performance on the GSE, you can talk to your high school counselor for more information.

Can I Take the Tests More Than Once?

No. Students are eligible to take each GSE only one time. For this reason, be sure that you are prepared to take the Golden State Examinations. If you are holding this book, you are well on your way!

How Can I Keep Track of All the GSE Tests and Requirements?

Determining which GSEs to take, and when to take them, can be a confusing process. The California Department of Education has designed some worksheets for use by students that will help you keep track of this information. Ask your high school counselor for a copy of these worksheets.

For additional information about the GSE program, contact the Standards, Curriculum, and Assessment Division of the California Department of Education:

Phone: (916) 657-3011
Fax: (916) 657-4964
Email: star@cde.ca.gov
Internet: www.cde.ca.gov/
 cilbranch/sca/gse/gse.html

How Do I Inform Colleges About My Golden State Awards?

If you are applying to a college, university, or military academy, you will want to make sure that any awards you received on the Golden State Examinations are included in your application. If you received high honors, honors, or recognition on a GSE, this will be noted on your high school transcript. In addition, you can get a form called the *GSE Status Report for College Applications*. This form is available from your high school counselor, and along with your high school transcript, it will ensure that admissions boards notice your performance on these tests.

HOW THIS BOOK IS ORGANIZED

The next chapter of this book is devoted to giving you the specifics about the test you are about to take. We will discuss test structure, format, and scoring, and we'll also talk about some techniques and strategies that can be helpful to you on the exam. Our goal is to provide you with a "bag of tricks" you can use throughout this exam.

We will then provide a specific content review of the subject material that's covered on the GSE. Rather than giving you lists of things to memorize, our goal is to give you an understanding of how the GSE works, what the test makers are looking for, and how to best attack the questions. How do we know what is tested on the GSEs? We have carefully studied California State Curriculum Standards and GSE questions, surveyed high school teachers, and reviewed textbooks to determine exactly what is covered on each test. We'll use sample questions throughout the review to show you how certain topics are tested on the GSE.

Finally, we have prepared and constructed *four* full-length practice tests for the Golden State Examination. We will provide you with detailed explanations to each problem, and sample written work, when appropriate. Use these tests to recognize the areas in which you need improvement.

WHO IS THE PRINCETON REVIEW?

The Princeton Review is the nation's leader in test preparation. We have offices in more than fifty cities across the country, as well as many outside the United States. The Princeton Review supports more than two million students every year with our courses, books, online services, and software programs. In addition to helping high school students prepare for the GSEs, we help them with the SAT-I, SAT-II, PSAT, and ACT, along with many other statewide standardized tests. The Princeton Review's strategies and techniques are unique and, most of all, successful.

Remember, this book will work best in combination with the material you have learned throughout your high school course. Our goals are to help you remember what you have been taught over the past year and show you how to apply this knowledge to the specific format and structure of the Golden State Examination.

AND FINALLY. . .

We applaud your efforts to spend the time and energy to prepare for the GSE in Algebra. You are giving yourself the opportunity to be rewarded for your academic achievement. Remember that the GSE will not test you on information you have never seen before. A strong year in your academic subject, combined with a review of the material and the test-taking strategies in this book will leave you more than prepared to handle the GSE. Don't become frustrated if you don't remember everything at once; it may take some time for the information and skills to come back.

Stay focused, practice, and try to have fun working through this book. And finally, good luck!

STRUCTURE AND STRATEGIES

It may seem pretty intimidating that only one-third of all students who take the GSEs receives any sort of honors. You might be wondering whether you can be one of them . . .but of course you can! Just remember that most students don't prepare at all before taking the GSEs, so you're already ahead of the game.

In this chapter, we'll tell you exactly which algebra concepts are tested, and how. We'll also give you an idea of the scoring process and the structure and format of the test. We'll also show you what you'll need to do to receive an Academic Excellence Award (high honors, honors, or recognition). It's crucial that you use our techniques when you're taking the test. We'll refer to these techniques throughout the book to make sure you incorporate them into your practice.

WHAT IS TESTED ON THE ALGEBRA GSE?

The content of the Algebra GSE is in alignment with the State Board *California Mathematics Academic Content Standards*. This means that what's tested on the Algebra GSE will be similar to the information you were presented during the academic year. Specifically, the following content areas are covered:

- **Algebraic Representation**

  You will need to be able to evaluate and simplify using real numbers. This will include using irrational numbers, radicals, scientific notation, factors, exponents, and patterns.

- **Solving Equations**

  In addition to solving equations, you will need to solve inequalities and systems of equations. Some of these problems will require you to factor, and have knowledge of absolute value and proportions.

- **Graphs of Relations and Functions**

  You will be responsible for recognizing the following functions: linear, quadratic, parallel lines, perpendicular lines, and coordinate geometry.

- **Geometric Relationships**

  You will need to know various geometric rules like perimeter, area, similarity, and the Pythagorean theorem.

- **Probability and Statistics**

  You will need knowledge of scattergrams, stem, and leaf plots.

- **Problem Solving**

  You will be asked to solve various algebra word problems. Some questions may involve modeling.

In the chapters ahead, we will cover each of the topics mentioned above. We will provide substantial review in each of the topic areas that will be covered on the Algebra GSE.

HOW IS THE ALGEBRA GSE EXAM STRUCTURED?

The GSE in Algebra is in two parts, administered in two 45-minute sections. For example, Part I may be on a Tuesday, and Part II on a Wednesday.

Part I consists of approximately thirty multiple-choice questions. These questions are designed to test a wide range of algebraic concepts. You will probably find several of these questions easy, but you may find that you are unfamiliar with the concepts tested in others. For example, many students don't have any geometry instruction until after their algebra class, but some concepts of geometry will be tested on the GSE. Don't worry, we'll review all the material you need to know.

In general, the multiple-choice questions emphasize the concepts and principles of algebra. Each of the questions consists of four answer choices. Later, we'll talk about how to use the answer choices to your advantage.

Part II consists of gridded response and written response questions. The gridded response questions will require you to solve problems; there will be no answer choices to choose from. You'll need to fill in your response on a grid found on your answer sheet. You can expect to see between five and ten of these questions on Part II. We'll cover gridded response questions throughout this book. The written response portion of Part II requires that you apply your mathematical skills; it's sort of a like an "algebra essay." You will be given a problem that involves several steps, and you'll be asked to write out a correct solution. You will be evaluated based on the explanations that accompany the solution, as well as the solution itself. This will be one area where you need to show your work in order to receive total credit.

HOW IS THE TEST SCORED?

A machine will score all of Part I and the gridded response questions in Part II. Mathematics teachers and other professionals will score the written response portion of the Algebra GSE.

Your performance on Part I, combined with your performance on Part II of the Algebra GSE will determine your overall score. It is important to note that the scoring criterion changes each time the test is administered. For this reason, we cannot give you specific information like, "You need to get 80 percent of the questions correct to receive a score of high honors."

CAN I USE A CALCULATOR ON THIS TEST?

Yes! A scientific or graphing calculator is required for some of the problems that are given on the Algebra GSE. You should use the calculator that you have used throughout your math classes. You can use any calculator you want, except for ones with QWERTY (typewriter) keyboards.

WHERE CAN I FIND A REAL GSE EXAM?

Sample copies of the real GSEs are not available, but you should get enough practice from the four full-length diagnostic tests in the back of this book, which are followed by explanations and sample student written responses. These tests simulate the format and kinds of questions you can expect to see on the GSE.

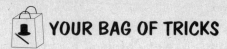

YOUR BAG OF TRICKS

Have you ever seen the cartoon *Felix the Cat*? Felix fought crime, solved problems, and got his way out of difficult situations by reaching into his bag of tricks. In this special bag, he'd find the exact tool he needed to resolve any situation. With his bag of tricks, Felix was invincible.

Throughout this book, we'll help you fill up your own bag of tricks. What will be in there? Strategies and tools for handling each type of question on the Algebra GSE, as well as general strategies for how to approach the test. It is important to know that being a smart test-taker is just as important as knowing the material tested. Managing your time, knowing when to guess, and knowing what the questions are *really* asking are skills you can learn, and we'll teach them to you. As you'll see, there is a difference between knowing the material, and being able to apply it to the test.

Let's take an example of two students, Gretchen and Laurie, each with the same amount of algebra knowledge. Now, Gretchen took the same math class as Laurie, but Gretchen has received additional training. She has learned to think like the people who write the GSE; she knows fast ways to eliminate incorrect answer choices, and has the best techniques to use for certain types of problems. In short, she has learned how to become a solid test-taker. Gretchen, with her bag of tricks, is now going to do much better on the GSE than Laurie. Why? Not because she knows more, but because she knows how to take this specific test in a smarter way than Laurie does. She understands the rules of the game. Once you know the rules of the game, you know how best to apply your skills to the game.

General Strategies

Now that you know what is tested on the Algebra GSE, and in what format it is tested, we need to talk about the best way to take this test. In the pages that follow, we'll discuss some general tools for you to use as you proceed through the test. Starting in Chapter 3, we will discuss specific strategies for particular *types* of questions.

An Empty Scantron Sheet is a Bad Scantron Sheet

In the past, you've probably taken a standardized test that had a guessing penalty. This penalty meant that points would be subtracted from your raw score if you answered a question incorrectly. Guessing penalties are meant to discourage test takers from answering every question. But guess what? There is *no* guessing penalty on the GSE! Your score is only determined by the number of questions that you get correct; it doesn't matter how many questions you get incorrect. So, when you take the GSE, there is one thing that you must do before you turn in your test: You must answer every single multiple-choice question. There are thirty questions on Part I of the Algebra GSE. Before you turn in your test, make sure that you have selected an answer for all thirty. Earning an Academic Excellence Award may boil down to just one additional point, and leaving a question blank guarantees a wrong answer.

So now you know that you must choose an answer for every question. Great, now let's talk about how to be an intelligent guesser.

 ## Process of Elimination (POE)

Try the following question:

What is the capital of Malawi?

Unsure? Do you know even where Malawi is located? If not, don't panic. Geography and world capitals are not topics tested on the GSE (especially the Algebra test!). If you had to answer this question without any answer choices, you'd probably be in trouble. You'd just randomly pick a city, and most likely guess wrong.

Of course, on the GSE, you will have answer choices to choose from. Rather than closing your eyes and selecting an answer at random, take a look at the choices—you might find some information that can help you:

What is the capital of Malawi?

A   Paris

B. Lilongwe

C. New York

D. London

Now do you know? Can you identify any answer choices that you know are *not* correct? Well, you can probably eliminate A, C, and D. Although you probably didn't know that Lilongwe was the capital of Malawi, you could tell that it was the correct answer by eliminating incorrect answer choices. This procedure is called Process of Elimination, or POE for short.

Process of Elimination will help you become a better guesser. This is because oftentimes, it's easier to see incorrect answer choices than it is to pinpoint the correct one. Remember to *cross out* any answer choice that you know is incorrect, then, if you still need to make a guess, select an answer from your remaining choices.

It is rare that POE will actually help you eliminate three answer choices like we did in the sample problem above. However, every time you get rid of one answer choice, the odds of getting that question correct go up significantly. Instead of a 25 percent chance of guessing correctly, you might find yourself guessing with a 50 percent (1 in 2) or 33 percent (1 in 3) chance of getting a question right.

Let's try another example that would be more likely to appear on the Algebra GSE:

> 1. Store X recently had a sale promoting a 20% discount on all items. If Teresa bought a dress originally priced at $64, what did she pay for the dress during the sale?
>
> A. $12.80
>
> B. $51.20
>
> C. $76.20
>
> D. $128.00

We'll review exactly how to answer equations that involve percentages, but for now, let's use POE on this question. Teresa is buying a dress on sale. If the dress was originally $64, then the price she paid for it should be less than $64. This means you can eliminate answer choices C and D. You may have already noticed that answer choice A was much, much lower than the original price, and eliminated it too. At worst, if you needed to make a guess on this question, it would be a fifty-fifty chance. Again, using POE will gain you points on the GSE.

Process of Elimination is such an important concept that we'll be referring to it throughout this book, including in the explanations provided to the practice tests. Some specific POE strategies will apply to certain geometry questions that will be presented in the chapters ahead. It is important that you practice using POE, because getting rid of incorrect answers is a powerful tool on the GSE.

You Don't Have to Start with Number 1

Some tests contain an order of difficulty within each section. On these kinds of tests, the first question is generally very easy, and the questions become progressively more difficult, with the last few questions being the hardest. On the Algebra GSE, however, there is no order of difficulty on the multiple-choice section of the exam. So doing the test straight through, from 1 to 30, may not be your best strategy. Your goal on the test is to work as rapidly as you can without sacrificing accuracy. This means that, if you find that a question is difficult for you, leave that one for later, and move on to another question.

The Two-Pass System

Have you ever been given a question that stumped you, but you were sure you could answer it? Have you ever said, "Just one more minute—I know I can figure this out!" Well, we all have, and we all know that one more minute sometimes means five more minutes, and often, we don't end up with the right answer at all.

Don't let one question ruin your whole day. You've got a certain number of questions to tackle, and allowing one to throw off your timing might set you back. Here is a general rule for the multiple-choice section: *If you haven't figured out the correct answer in 90 seconds, skip the question and come back to it later.* We're not telling you to give up on it—if you can't answer the question, make a small mark on your answer sheet so you can come back to it later. After you complete the section, go back to the questions you weren't able to solve. Remember to use POE on these questions, and make sure you have selected an answer choice for every question before time is up.

We call this strategy the two-pass system. The first time you go through a section, try every question. If a question seems too difficult or stumps you, move right along. Once you've completed the section, go back to those questions. If you still aren't sure how to solve them, use POE and then make a guess.

Oftentimes, when you go back to a problem a second time you'll have a revelation about how to solve it. (We've all left a test and said, "Oh yeah! Now I know what the answer to number 5 was.") Skipping the problem and then going back to it might give you a chance to have this revelation *during* the test, when it will still be useful.

Provide Explanations on Written Response Questions

Many students think the written response section of the Algebra GSE is the most difficult part of the exam. Later in the book, we will spend time practicing exactly how to approach these written response questions, so that you'll be comfortable with them by the time test day comes. For now, you only need to remember this about answering a written response question: Write out everything you do clearly, and provide explanations!

To receive a high score on the written response section, you will need to provide explanations for the material you present. If you aren't sure about your answer, make sure you explain any rules you used to make your calculations. You can receive a lot of partial credit on this section for providing sound explanations, even if you don't end up with the correct answer. Students who leave things blank because they aren't sure of the answer will cost themselves lots of points on this section. The reverse is also true: Students may give a correct answer but still lose points for not providing a complete explanation. This is one area in which showing your work is not only helpful, it is vital to scoring well.

We will discuss strategies for the written response questions in greater detail as we move through the review of geometry concepts.

YOU ARE IN CONTROL

We know that taking the Algebra GSE can be a stressful process. With all this built-up pressure, it might feel like this test is totally out of your control. But, the opposite is true—you are in control. Although you can't decide what number pencil to bring to the exam (you must bring a #2) or where to sit during the test, you can decide how you take the GSE. So let's review what we've discussed in this chapter:

- First, you can take advantage of the multiple-choice format of Part I. There is no guessing penalty, and you can use Process of Elimination to add points to your score, even without knowing the correct answer.

- Second, you can answer the multiple-choice questions in any order you want. Spend time with questions that you're comfortable with. If question 12 is really stumping you, move on to question 13 and return to 12 later.

- Third, you can gain points on the written response section by providing clear explanations. Sometimes, mentioning a definition or rule can help you gain additional points, even if you do not know the correct answer.

As you build upon your knowledge of algebra by reviewing the chapters ahead, you'll gain more confidence in your ability to handle the exam.

 ## BAG OF TRICKS SUMMARY

Here is a list of the tricks you'll find in your bag of tricks—be sure to make good use of them.

- Process of Elimination (POE)

- Leave no question blank

- 90 seconds per question limit

- On the written response questions, provide explanations.

Now let's begin the algebra review.

Part II

THE BASICS
OF ALGEBRA

OVERVIEW

Throughout the next few chapters, we will review all of the different types of questions that could appear on the Algebra GSE. As you move forward in our review, the questions will become more complex. Before we start reviewing the specific types of questions tested on the Algebra GSE, you should be certain that you are familiar with some basic terms and concepts that you'll need to know for this test. The material is not very difficult, and the sample problems are not representative of actual test questions, but you must know this information backwards and forwards. If you don't, you'll lose valuable points on the test, and have trouble setting problems up correctly. If you find that you are comfortable with this material, great! You will be well on your way to mastering this exam.

In this chapter, we will integrate a review of math basics with a review of algebra. If you have additional questions, we recommend using an additional resource book, such as *Math Smart* by Marcia Lerner, published by The Princeton Review.

VARIABLES—THE SYMBOLS USED IN ALGEBRA

Algebra is a type of mathematics in which letters represent numbers. Before your first algebra class, you used numbers to describe all mathematical relationships, but in algebra, these letters (called **variables**) are introduced, seemingly to complicate your life. If you think about it, the word describes what it does—a variable is not a fixed value; it does, in fact, vary. The value of a variable is determined by the other numbers and variables that are included in an equation. Before we discuss an equation, let's flash back all the way to when you were first learning to add two numbers.

EXPRESSIONS

What's 4 + 3? 7, of course. You can use the number line to help you add. When you add two positive numbers, you are simply counting to the right on a number line. In our example, we count 4 spaces to the right, and then another three spaces, giving us 7 total spaces to the right.

$$4 + 3 = 7$$

The phrase 4 + 3 is a numeric expression. Imagine if we replaced one of these numbers with a variable: $4 + x$. Now this is called **an algebraic expression**. We can replace the variable with a number in order to evaluate the algebraic expression. For example:

Evaluate $4 + x$ for $x = 5$

Here, we substitute the 5 wherever we see x in the expression above.

$$4 + x$$

$$4 + 5 = 9$$

The statement above, 4 + 5 = 9, is an **equation**. It sets one set of numbers equal to another set of numbers. Through a series of operations, we can relate numbers to each other to create an equation. Equations are fundamental to the study of algebra.

So what exactly is an equation? A dictionary definition would probably read like this: An equation is a mathematical statement that uses an equal sign to state that two expressions represent the same number or are equivalent. But all you need to know is this: **An equation is a statement in which the value of the left side equals the value of the right side.**

Let's go back to our first example:

4 + 3 = 7 is an equation (sometimes called a **true equation**).

$4 + x = 7$ is an algebraic equation.

Now we will review how to solve equations that include variables, but first. . .

Simplifying Expressions

Remember what a factor is? **Factors** of a number are defined as numbers that divide evenly into that number. For example, the factors of 24 are: 1, 2, 3, 4, 6, 8, 12, and 24.

If you are asked to find the factors of a number, the best way to make sure you don't leave any out is to find them in pairs and start with 1 and the number, going up to 2 and trying it, and working that way. For instance, if you are asked to find the factors of 36, start with: 1, 36, and then the next pair: 2, 18; then 3, 12; then 4, 9; 5 doesn't work; 6 does (6, 6); 7 doesn't work; 8 doesn't work; when you get to 9—you've already written it down, so you know you're done.

Thus, the factors of 36 are 1, 2, 3, 4, 6, 9, 12, 18, and 36.

Factors are helpful for **reducing** expressions, like fractions. A fraction can be expressed in many different ways. For example,

$$\frac{50}{100} = \frac{25}{50} = \frac{10}{20} = \frac{4}{8} = \frac{2}{4} = \frac{1}{2}$$

When you add or multiply fractions, you will often end up with a couple of really big numbers in the numerator and denominator. You will need to know how to reduce fractions like these to their simplest value. To reduce a fraction, divide both the **numerator** (the top part of the fraction) and the **denominator** (the bottom part of the fraction) by an equal amount. This process may take several steps. While it may save time to find the largest number that will divide into both numbers, try to keep your pencil moving. Don't worry about whether two numbers will both divide by 24! Start with nice, small numbers. See if both parts of the fraction will divide by 2, 3, or 5. If you find that you need to reduce again, fine, you'll still get the result quickly. Let's look at the following fraction:

$\frac{12}{60}$. What can we divide both numbers by? If you recognized 12, good—the fraction will reduce to $\frac{1}{5}$. But if not, don't panic; start with an easy number.

Both 12 and 60 are even, so start with 2. This will give you $\frac{6}{30}$. Now try 3, and you're down to $\frac{2}{10}$. Divide by 2 again, and you've got $\frac{1}{5}$. It took a few more steps, but we got the correct answer nonetheless. If possible, try to reduce fractions before performing operations with them. This will save you time and help you avoid errors that come up when you start to manipulate large numbers.

We talked about factors and reducing fractions so that you can see how these processes work in algebra. They are involved in a procedure known as simplifying expressions. In the same way that we want to keep fractions in their reduced form, we always want algebraic expressions to be in their simplest form. You can simplify algebraic expressions by using a few basic rules, and the same methods we used above with regular numbers. Here's an example:

Simplify the following expression: $\dfrac{12ab}{6a}$

Here's How to Crack It

To simplify this expression, you want to find things that the denominator and numerator have in common. You can think of what we did with the fractions in the problems above—we looked for common factors. So what factors are in common here? Let's rewrite this expression in its components:

$$\frac{12 \cdot a \cdot b}{6 \cdot a}$$

Now we can eliminate things that the top and bottom part of the fraction have in common. For example, the variable a is in both the top and bottom, so eliminate it. Next, notice that 6 is a common factor between 12 and 6—so reduce the numerical fraction. The correctly reduced expression looks like this:

$$\frac{12 \cdot a \cdot b}{6 \cdot a} = 2b$$

In short, to simplify, look for common factors in algebraic expressions. Your algebra teacher may have taught you things like the identity property, or the commutative property. Don't worry about learning those rules again—just be sure you know how to simplify algebraic expressions.

WRITING EXPRESSIONS USING ALGEBRA

Many word problems on the Algebra GSE can be solved easily if you translate them into algebraic expressions. In the chapters ahead, we will work on solving word problems, but here you'll learn to translate certain word phrases into algebra. Let's start by looking at a few different expressions:

- **8 more than a number**

  Here, the word *more* tells us that this will be an addition problem (words like *more*, *sum* or *greater than* are indicators that the problem will involve addition). The correct algebraic representation of this phrase is $x + 8$. If you want to test yourself, choose a number, like 4. 4 + 8 = 12. Does 8 more than 4 equal 12? Yes, so *8 more than a number* means $x + 8$.

- **5 less than a number**

  The phrase *less than* tells us that this is a subtraction problem (words like *less than*, *difference*, or *fewer*, indicate a subtraction problem). The correct algebraic representation for this phrase is $x - 5$.

- **The product of 7 and a number**

  This phrase tells us that this is a multiplication problem (words like *product* and *times* can be used to indicate a multiplication problem). The correct answer is $7 \times x$, or simply $7x$.

- **A number divided by 4**

  The phrase *divided by* indicates that this is a division problem. The correct representation is $\frac{x}{4}$.

MATH FLASHBACKS

Now we'll review some arithmetic rules that will be crucial in making sure you can solve equations.

The Number Line

The number line is a two-dimensional way of looking at the relationship between positive and negative numbers.

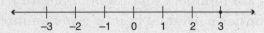

A **positive** number is any number that is located to the right of zero on the number line. Positive numbers are greater than zero. **Negative** numbers are located to the left of zero on the number line, and are less than zero. What about zero? Zero is neither positive nor negative.

Positive numbers get larger the further they move away from zero on the number line. For example, 15 is larger than 2—it is farther away from zero on the number line. For negative numbers, a number gets *smaller* the farther it is from zero on the number line. For example, −4 is smaller than −3. It may seem strange, but it's true.

Combining Positive and Negative Numbers

What if we wanted to find the sum of 6 and −2 (remember, sum means addition)? To do this, count six spaces to the right of zero on the number line (our positive 6). To add −2, count over two spaces to the left. Where did you stop? 4, so 6 + (−2) = 4.

Adding a negative number is the same thing as subtracting a positive number. This means that we could rewrite the addition problem above in this way:

$$6 - 2 = 4$$

Visualize the number line to help you work with positive and negative numbers, or even draw one out.

Positive and Negative Numbers—Multiplication Rules

Here are a few rules to remember when multiplying positive and negative numbers together:

1. positive × positive = positive

2. negative × negative = positive

3. positive × negative = negative

Integers

Integers are a specific type of number, also known as whole numbers. They are "whole" in that they are not fractions or decimals. Some examples of integers are: 1, 2, 3, 4, 400, 389, 27, and –912. Zero is also an integer. We can break up the group of integers into positive integers (1, 2, 3, . . .) and negative integers (–1, –2, –3, –4 . . .). So now, what *isn't* an integer? Here are a few examples:

$$2.7, \frac{-33}{2}, 27.246857, \text{ and } \pi$$

Essentially, integers are numbers that do not contain fractions or decimals. If a number is a fraction or has a decimal in it, it is *not* an integer.

Odd and Even Numbers

The terms **odd** and **even** are used to describe certain types of integers. Even numbers are integers that can be divided evenly by 2. Examples of even numbers are:

$$-24, -2, 0, 4, 8, 12, 416, \text{ etc.}$$

One way to tell if a number is even is to look at the last digit. An integer is even if its last digit is even. That is, any integer that ends in 0, 2, 4, 6, or 8 is an even number. –357982 is even, because its last digit (2) is an even number.

Odd numbers are integers that cannot be divided evenly by 2. Examples of odd numbers are: –25, –3, 1, 3, 5, 7, 9, and 9245. One way to tell if a number is odd is to look at the last digit. An integer is odd if its last digit is odd. For example, –444,225 is an odd number, because the last digit (5) is an odd number; it can't be divided by 2.

Notice that zero is an even number (remember that zero is neither positive nor negative).

Here are some rules that deal with the results of combining even and odd numbers:

1. even × even = even

2. odd × odd = odd

3. even × odd = even

4. even + even = even

5. odd + odd = even

6. even + odd = odd

While it is helpful to have these rules memorized, you can always recreate them by trying some examples yourself. For example, if you multiply 2 and 4 together (two even numbers), you get 8, also an even number. Therefore, you know that even × even = an even number. These rules hold true no matter what values you choose.

Places and Digits

Digits are used to create numbers, just as the alphabet is used to create words. There are ten digits: 0, 1, 2, 3, 4, 5, 6, 7, 8, 9. The number 324,856 is made up of six different digits. Each of these digits is in a **place**. A place indicates where the digit is located within the number. Let's use the following number to review the places of a number:

$$243.789$$

The 2 is in the hundreds place. Its value is $2 \times 100 = 200$

The 4 is in the tens place. Its value is $4 \times 10 = 40$

The 3 is in the units place. Its value is $3 \times 1 = 3$

The 7 is in the tenths place. It has a value of $\frac{7}{10}$, or .7

The 8 is in the hundredths place. It has a value of $\frac{8}{100}$, or .08

The 9 is in the thousandths place. It has a value of $\frac{9}{1000}$, or .009

Arithmetic Operations

There are only a few **arithmetic operations** that are tested on the Algebra GSE:

1. addition ($4 + 8 = 12$)

2. subtraction ($12 - 8 = 4$)

3. multiplication ($4 \times 8 = 32$ or $4 \cdot 8 = 32$)

4. division ($32 \div 4 = 8$)

5. raising to a power ($2^2 = 4$)

6. finding a square root ($\sqrt{25} = 5$)

There will be a brief review of these operations in the next few pages.

You are probably very familiar with the first four math operations. When you use these operations, the results each have a special name:

1. The result of addition is a **sum**.

2. The result of subtraction is a **difference**.

3. The result of multiplication is a **product**.

4. The result of division is a **quotient**.

But in equations, how do you know in what order to perform these operations?

PEMDAS

Let's say you wanted to solve the following expression:

$$6 + \frac{10}{5} - 3 \cdot 2 + (3 \cdot 5)$$

There are a number of different operations that we need to perform to simplify this expression, but these operations must be performed in a specific order. What is the order? Simply put, it's

PEMDAS

This acronym stands for the following math operations: Parenthesis, Exponents, Multiplication, Division, Addition, and Subtraction. In any expression, the first thing you solve is the operation inside parentheses; next, perform any operations involving exponents; then, perform all multiplication and division at the same time, going from left to right in the expression; finally, perform all addition and subtraction, again going from left to right in the expression. Many students have learned this as **P**lease **E**xcuse **M**y **D**ear **A**unt **S**ally (although no one seems to know the story behind that phrase . . .).

Most test questions will be designed so that you have a clear understanding of the order in which you must perform the operations. However, if you are unsure of exactly in what order to solve a problem, be sure to use the rules of PEMDAS.

Let's go back to the expression above, and solve it using PEMDAS:

$$6 + \frac{10}{5} - 3 \cdot 2 + \left(3 \cdot 5\right)$$

Step 1: Do all work inside the parenthesis. $3 \times 5 = 15$, so our problem now looks like this:

$$6 + \frac{10}{5} - 3 \cdot 2 + 15$$

Step 2: There are no exponents, so we move to multiplication and division, moving from left to right in the expression:

$$6 + 2 - 6 + 15$$

Step 3: We finish the problem by doing the addition and subtraction, moving from left to right:

$$8 - 6 + 15$$

$$2 + 15$$

$$17$$

Exponents

Exponents are a shorthand way of simplifying a series of multiplied numbers. For example, we can use exponents to simplify the following expression:

$$3 \times 3 \times 3 \times 3 \times 3 \times 3 \times 3 \times 3$$

In the expression above, we are told to multiply the number 3 a total of eight times. This common number, 3, is called the base. The number of times we multiply it (8) is called the power.

The correct exponential form to the expression above is 3^8.

Now, we can use exponents with algebra, in order to simplify algebraic expressions. For example:

$$a \cdot a \cdot a \cdot a \cdot a \cdot a \cdot a \cdot a$$

This expression multiplies the variable a, 8 times. Using exponents, we can rewrite this expression as a^8.

Combining Exponents

So we use exponents to provide a shorthand way to represent multiplication — this can help us summarize a series of operations with a single base number and exponent. Now we're going to review how to combine exponents, which will allow you to simplify numerical expressions even further.

Exponents must have the same base in order to be combined. For example, we can combine 8^3 and 8^5 because both terms have a base of 8. We cannot combine 3^8 and 5^8 using exponents because each term has a different base.

Let's start with the rule of multiplying: *When multiplying two exponents with the same base together, add the exponents.*

Therefore,

$$8^3 \times 8^5 = 8^8$$

Likewise,

$$a^3 \times a^5 = a^8$$

And here's the rule for the division of exponents (with the same base): *When dividing two exponents with the same base, subtract the exponents.*

Therefore,

$$\frac{3^6}{3^2} = 3^4$$

Likewise,

$$\frac{a^7}{a} = a^6$$

Now use what you've learned to simplify the following expression:

$$\frac{(a^3 b^6)(a^2 b^7)}{a^2 b^4}$$

Here's How to Crack It

You first need to use the rules of PEMDAS to simplify this expression. Start by combining exponents that have the same base, as follows:

$$\frac{(a^3 b^6)(a^2 b^7)}{a^2 b^4} = \frac{a^5 b^{13}}{a^2 b^4}$$

Now you can simplify further by dividing the terms using the rule for dividing exponents:

$$\frac{(a^5 b^{13})}{a^2 b^4} = a^3 b^9$$

and $a^3 b^9$ is reduced.

Raising an Exponent to a Power

What would happen if we put an exponent on top of an exponent? For example, what if you were asked to multiply this series of values:

$$3x^2 \cdot 3x^2 \cdot 3x^2 \cdot 3x^2 \cdot 3x^2 \cdot 3x^2 \cdot 3x^2$$

Here the same value is multiplied seven times. To simplify this expression, we could write $(3x^2)^7$; this means that the phrase $(3x^2)$ is raised to the seventh power. If we wanted to simplify this, we would follow the rule on raising exponents to a power: *When raising an exponent to another power, multiply the exponents.*

Therefore, the value of $(3x^2)^7$ is $3^7 \cdot x^{14}$. Notice how we raise every value inside the parenthesis to the power, including the **coefficient** (the number before the variable). Here are a few more examples for practice:

$$(y^5)^3 = y^{15}$$

$$(2x^3)^2 = 4x^6$$

$$(m^3)^3 = m^9$$

$$\left(\frac{3}{4}\right)^2 = \frac{3^2}{4^2} = \frac{9}{16}$$

(Notice that when you raise a fraction to a power, both the top and the bottom part of the fraction are raised to that power.)

If you are ever confused about what to do with exponents, write them out. This leads to the helpful reminder about exponents: *when in doubt, write it out.*

Absolute Value

The absolute value of a number is its distance from 0 on the number line. The line symbols $|x|$ are used to represent absolute value. For example, the number 5 is five units away from 0 on the number line. The number –5 is also five units away from 0 on the number line. Therefore,

$$|5| = 5 \text{ and } |{-5}| = 5$$

To calculate absolute value, simply take the positive value of the number that appears inside the absolute value symbol.

Now let's take a look at how absolute value works with an algebraic expression. Consider the following expression:

$$|2x - 4|$$

What is the absolute value of this expression if $x = 3$. What about if $x = 1$?

$$\text{If } x = 3: |2(3) - 4| = |6 - 4| = |2| = 2$$

$$\text{If } x = 1: |2(1) - 4| = |2 - 4| = |{-2}| = 2$$

When you are given an algebraic expression contained within an absolute value, be sure to completely evaluate the expression before worrying about the absolute value. For example, if you were asked to evaluate the absolute value of an expression in which $x = -2$, you would not change the value of –2, you would only change the value of the overall expression, at the end.

The Distributive Property

Are the following expressions equivalent?

$$(2 \times 5) + (2 \times 8) \text{ and } 2 \times (5 + 8)$$

The two values may look similar to you, and you could use a calculator to find that each one will give you the value of 26. The **distributive property** of multiplication tells us that expressions like the one above are equivalent. We can summarize this rule with the following algebraic equation: For any numbers, x, y, and z,

$$x(y + z) = xy + xz$$

The distributive property can also be used in reverse:

$$xy + xz = x(y + z)$$

You will find this very helpful in factoring equations, which we will discuss in the chapters ahead.

Multiples

Multiples are defined as numbers that your original number will divide into evenly. For example, the multiples of 4 are 4, 8, 12, 16, 20, 24, etc. One way to remember multiples is to think of your "times tables." To find the multiples of 4, start with 4×1 (4), then 4×2 (8), 4×3 (12), etc.

Students often have trouble remembering the difference between factors and multiples. When you think of factors, think of fractions, or the smaller pieces of a number; when you are asked to find multiples, think of multiplying, and use the times tables to calculate the multiples.

What are the multiples of 12? They are 12, 24, 36, 48 . . .

What are the *factors* of 12? They're 1, 2, 3, 4, 6, and 12.

Fractions

Adding and Subtracting Fractions That Have the Same Denominator

To add two or more fractions that have the same denominator, simply add the numerators of the fractions. The final denominator will be the common denominator. Here is an example:

$$\frac{3}{4} + \frac{1}{4} = \frac{3 + 1}{4} = \frac{4}{4} = 1$$

Subtraction works in exactly the same way:

$$\frac{3}{4} - \frac{1}{4} = \frac{3 - 1}{4} = \frac{2}{4} = \frac{1}{2}$$

Converting Mixed Numbers to Fractions

On this test, you may find mixed numbers—that is, numbers that contain both a whole number and a fraction. An example of a mixed number is $3\frac{4}{5}$. When you come across a mixed number, you should convert it into a fraction (often referred to as an **improper fraction**, since the numerator will be greater than the denominator). Let's convert $3\frac{4}{5}$ into a standard fraction.

First, convert the integer into a fraction that has the same denominator as the fraction in the mixed number. In this example, we want to turn the integer 3 into a fraction with a denominator of 5:

$$3 = \frac{3}{1} = \frac{15}{5}$$

Next, add the two fractions with a common denominator together:

$$\frac{15}{5} + \frac{4}{5} = \frac{19}{5}$$

Converting mixed numbers into fractions will help make your calculations easier. You can also do it this way. Starting with $3\frac{4}{5}$, $5 \cdot 3 = 15 + 4 = 19$, and put that number over the starting denominator. That's easier.

 The Bowtie

Unfortunately, not all fraction problems will contain fractions that have the same denominator, but there is a way to add and subtract fractions with different denominators.

Welcome to the **Bowtie**. The Bowtie is a powerful tool that will simplify the process of adding, subtracting, and comparing fractions with unequal denominators. Here's how it works:

$$\frac{1}{2} + \frac{3}{4}$$

$$\overset{4}{\frac{1}{2}} \underset{+}{\times} \overset{6}{\frac{3}{4}}$$

$$\frac{10}{8}$$

The first step is to multiply in the directions of each arrow. Write each number above the fraction at the top of the arrow. Next, use the sign (in this case addition) to combine the two numbers you just wrote down. In the example above, we added 4 and 6 together, giving us 10 as the numerator. In order to find the denominator, multiply the two denominators together, which gives us 8. The fraction is $\frac{10}{8}$.

The beauty of the Bowtie is that you don't have to sit there trying to come up with a common denominator. Simply multiply twice, add, multiply again, and you're done! Oh yeah, it's called the Bowtie because the arrows in the problem look like a bowtie.

Now that we know how to combine fractions, let's do a problem involving mixed numbers:

> Lynn is filling an aquarium. After she pours $1\frac{3}{4}$ gallons of water into the tank, the tank contains a total of $2\frac{1}{5}$ gallons of water. How much water was in the tank before Lynn added the water?
>
> A. $\frac{9}{20}$
>
> B. $\frac{11}{20}$
>
> C. $\frac{17}{20}$
>
> D. $1\frac{11}{20}$

Here's How to Crack it

First convert the mixed numbers into fractions so that you can subtract the two fractional amounts. The first mixed number, $1\frac{3}{4}$, converts to the fraction $\frac{7}{4}$, and the second mixed number, $2\frac{1}{5}$, converts to the fraction $\frac{11}{5}$. Next we want to find the difference between the total amount of water in the tank and the amount of water that was just added. Our expression now looks like:

$$\frac{11}{5} - \frac{7}{4} =$$

To find the difference, use the Bowtie. $11 \times 4 = 44$, and $5 \times 7 = 35$. $44 - 35$ gives us 9 as the numerator. The denominator is 5 3 4, or 20, and the difference between the two fractions is $\frac{9}{20}$. Choice A is the correct answer.

Multiplying Fractions

To multiply fractions, line them up and multiply both the numerator and denominator straight across:

$$\frac{4}{5} \cdot \frac{5}{6} = \frac{20}{30}$$

We performed one multiplication problem above another. Across the top of the fractions, we multiplied 4 and 5; across the bottom of the fractions, we multiplied 5 and 6.

However, there is an even easier way to solve the fraction problem above. When multiplying two fractions, always look to see if you can reduce either or both of the starting fractions. In the problem above, we could cancel out the five in each fraction—that would leave us with a 4 on the top left and a 6 on the bottom right. We can reduce these numbers by two, leaving us with $\frac{2}{3}$, the final answer. In general, your calculations will be easier if you take a second to reduce before you multiply.

Dividing Fractions

Dividing fractions requires one more step than does multiplying fractions. To divide one fraction by another, flip the second fraction over, and multiply (in fancier terms, multiply by the reciprocal of the second term). So your first step in a fraction division problem is to turn it into a multiplying fraction problem. Here is an example:

$$\frac{\frac{4}{5}}{\frac{3}{10}} = \left(\frac{4}{5}\right)\left(\frac{10}{3}\right)$$

We can reduce the 10 and the 5, and get the result $\frac{8}{3}$.

Make sure that you reduce only *after* you have flipped the second fraction. Also, sometimes students get confused when whole numbers are involved, such as

$$\frac{6}{\frac{2}{3}}$$

Remember, a whole number can be a fraction; just place the whole number over 1. In this problem, we have $\dfrac{\frac{6}{1}}{\frac{2}{3}}$. Flip the second fraction to get $\left(\dfrac{6}{1}\right)\left(\dfrac{3}{2}\right)$.

The answer is $\dfrac{18}{2}$, or 9.

Comparing Fractions

The Algebra GSE sometimes contains problems that require you to identify which of two fractions is larger. When fractions have the same denominator, it is easy to tell which amount is bigger. For example, which fraction is larger, $\dfrac{1}{4}$ or $\dfrac{3}{4}$? The answer is $\dfrac{3}{4}$. 3 parts out of 4 is clearly larger than 1 part out of 4.

When two fractions have the same denominator, simply choose the fraction with the largest numerator.

Comparing fractions becomes more difficult when they do not have a common denominator. Which fraction is greater, $\dfrac{4}{7}$ or $\dfrac{3}{5}$? Well, the most efficient way to compare these fractions is to use the Bowtie. Here we'll use the first step of the Bowtie—cross multiply as the arrows indicate below:

$$\overset{20}{}\overset{}{}\overset{21}{}$$
$$\dfrac{4}{7}\diagdown\!\!\!\!\!\diagup\dfrac{3}{5}$$

The result of 4×5 is 20, so we write this above the fraction $\dfrac{4}{7}$; the other arrow gives us 21. Now compare the two products we just calculated. The one on the right is bigger. Since 21 is the larger product, the fraction underneath, $\dfrac{3}{5}$, is the larger fraction! Once again, the bowtie will save you time when you're working with fractions. This is much more efficient than turning these fractions into decimals, or even finding a common denominator.

Those Tricky Fractions

So now we've reviewed how to perform all basic operations with fractions. By using the bowtie, you can add, subtract, and compare fractions with ease, and we've also reviewed the rules of multiplication and division with fractions.

And as you may have noticed, sometimes, the result of a fraction problem doesn't seem to make sense. Here are a few things to remember with fractions: *Multiplying two fractions will yield a product that's less than the original fractions.*

Generally, when we think of multiplying two numbers, we think of the product as being larger than what we started with, for example, $10 \cdot 7 = 70$, but $\left(\frac{1}{10}\right)\left(\frac{1}{7}\right) = \frac{1}{70}$, a number that's much smaller than either $\frac{1}{10}$ or $\frac{1}{7}$.

Also, pay close attention when identifying the largest fraction. It is extremely easy to recognize that 6 is greater than 2, but you must remember that $\frac{1}{6}$ is much *less* than $\frac{1}{2}$. If you are unsure as to which fraction is largest, use the Bowtie.

Decimals

As we mentioned earlier, fractions are simply a way to indicate division. Fractions can also be expressed as **decimals**; you can convert any fraction into a decimal. You probably know some already ($\frac{1}{2} = .5$; $\frac{1}{4} = .25$). To find the decimal equivalent of a fraction, simply divide the numerator by the denominator. For example,

$$\frac{3}{4} = 3 \div 4 = .75$$

Adding and Subtracting Decimals

To add or subtract decimals, you must first align the decimal places of all the numbers. Then, simply add or subtract.

$$
\begin{array}{r}
2.72 \\
+ \ 3.46 \\
\hline
6.18
\end{array}
\qquad
\begin{array}{r}
8.19 \\
- \ 1.54 \\
\hline
6.65
\end{array}
$$

If you are trying to add or subtract two decimals, and the two numbers do not have the same number of digits, you will need to add zero's to fill out the places in each number. For example, if we want to find the difference between 8.3 and 3.784, we first need to set up the problem:

$$\begin{array}{r} 8.3 \\ -\ 2.784 \\ \hline \end{array}$$

To be able to subtract from the top number, add zeros to the right of the 3—in the hundredths and thousandths place. The problem now looks like this:

$$\begin{array}{r} 8.300 \\ -\ 2.784 \\ \hline 5.516 \end{array}$$

Multiplying Decimals

The best way to multiply decimals is to ignore the decimal points until you have completed the multiplication. Once you've multiplied, count the number of digits that are located to the right of all decimal points. Then place the decimal point that number of places to the left of your answer. Take a look at the following example:

$$\begin{array}{r} 2.45 \\ \times\ 3.42 \\ \hline 490 \\ 7350 \\ \hline 7840 \end{array}$$

Collectively, there are three numbers located to the right of the decimal point, so we need to put the decimal point in our answer, three places to the left. Starting with the 0, count over three places to the left. The answer is 7.840.

Dividing Decimals

When diving decimals, you need to make sure that the divisor (the number you are dividing by) is a whole number. For example, if you are given the problem

$$\frac{1.86}{.3}$$

you must first turn the .3 into a whole number. In order to make .3 a whole number, you would want to move the decimal point one place to the right, but *whatever you do to the bottom part of the fraction, you must do to the top!* This means that you need to move the decimal point in 1.86 one place to the right, which gives you 18.6. Now the division problem looks like this:

$$\frac{18.6}{3} = 6.2$$

Percents

Percents are very similar to fractions and decimals. In fact, a percent is really just a fraction whose denominator is 100. The word "percent" means *out of 100*.

$$50\% = \frac{50}{100} = .5$$

$$47\% = \frac{47}{100} = .47$$

As you can see, percents can be converted into fractions and decimals, and vice versa. In order to convert a fraction into a percent, the easiest thing to do is to first convert the fraction into a decimal. Then multiply the decimal by 100. For example:

$$\frac{3}{4} = (3 \div 4) = .75(100) = 75\%$$

$$\frac{6}{10} = (6 \div 10) = .6(100) = 60\%$$

This process will work for any fraction, but it does require a few steps. On the Algebra GSE, there are a few fractions that might show up several times. Here are ones that appear so often you should memorize them:

FRACTION	DECIMAL	PERCENT
$\frac{1}{100}$	.01	1%
$\frac{1}{8}$	.125	12.5%
$\frac{1}{5}$	.2	20%
$\frac{1}{4}$	.25	25%
$\frac{1}{3}$	.333	$33\frac{1}{3}$%
$\frac{2}{5}$	.4	40%
$\frac{1}{2}$	.5	50%
$\frac{3}{5}$	.6	60%
$\frac{2}{3}$	.667	$66\frac{2}{3}$%
$\frac{3}{4}$	.75	75%
$\frac{4}{5}$	.8	80%

Breaking Down Percent Questions

If you can break down a percent question, oftentimes you will find it easier to approximate the answer—sometimes you can even use POE to choose the correct response, without doing lengthy computations! This is how it would work. Try simplifying the following problem:

What is 23% of 520?

Let's start with an easy percent to approximate, like 10%. To find 10% of a number, simply move the decimal point one place to the left. So 10% of 520 = 52. Since we are looking for a number that's greater than 20%, just multiply 52 by 2 to get 20% of 520, which is $2 \times 52 = 104$.

To find 1% of any number, all you have to do is move the decimal point of that number over two places to the left. In our example, 1% of 520 = 5.2. Since we want 3%, multiply 5.2 by 3 to get 15.6.

Now, we can combine the values to find the correct answer. 20% of 520 = 104, and 3% of 520 = 15.6. So 23% of 520 = 104 + 15.6, or 119.6. With a little practice, you'll find that you'll be able to solve percentage questions with minimal calculation. Here's an example:

A school district is proposing a 15% decrease in the number of students per classroom. Currently there are 20 students per classroom. How many students per classroom would there be with the proposed decrease?

A. 23 students

B. 19 students

C. 18.5 students

D. 17 students

Here's How to Crack It

We need to find 15% of 20. Using the techniques discussed above, we can break down this 15% into 10% and 5%. 10% of 20 is 2. Half of that is 1. Thus, 15% of 20 is 2 + 1, or 3 students. Since the school district is proposing to decrease the number of students, subtract. The new total would be 20 − 3 = 17. D is the correct answer.

Translating Percents

Many percent questions will be in the form of word problems. To set up these problems correctly, you'll need to be able to translate percent problem words into their mathematical equivalents. Hearken back to the section called Writing Expressions Using Algebra, and refresh your memory a bit before learning these new translations.

Of =   Multiply   ($\frac{1}{3}$ of 24 $= \frac{1}{3} \times 24$)

Percent =   # out of 100   (30 percent $= \frac{30}{100}$ or 30%)

What =	Variable	(30 percent of what $= \frac{30}{100} \times x$)

Is, are, were =   Equals Sign   ($\frac{1}{3}$ of 24 is $= \frac{1}{3} \times 24$)

Here's an example:

> Teresa took a science test that had 40 questions. If she answered seven questions, and left nine unanswered, what percent of the questions did Teresa answer correctly?
>
> A. 9%
>
> B. 16%
>
> C. 40%
>
> D. 60%

Here's How to Crack It

To set up a math equation for the above problem, translate the last sentence.

What percent	translates to	$\frac{x}{100}$
of the questions	translates to	$\times 40$
did she answer correctly?	translates to	$= 24$ (the number of questions correct can be found by subtracting 7 and 9 from 40).

So the equation reads:

$$\frac{x}{100} \times 40 = 24$$

Now, we can manipulate the equation to find the percent:

$$\frac{x}{100} \times 40 = 24$$

$$\frac{x}{100} = \frac{24}{40}$$

$$\frac{x}{100} = \frac{3}{5}$$

$$x = 60$$

D is the correct answer.

Ballparking, as always, is helpful on this problem. If you recognized that Teresa answered more than half of the questions correctly, then only one answer choice, D, will work.

Percent Change

Some algebra questions will ask you to find a percent increase or decrease between two values, or you may be asked what percent different, one number is from another. In either case, you should use the percent change formula:

$$\% \text{ change} = \frac{\text{difference}}{\text{original amount}}$$

Here's an example:

> In 1998, Company X sold a total of 40,000 computers. In 1999, Company X sold a total of 50,000 computers. By what percent did sales of computers increase for Company X from 1998 to 1999?
>
> A. 20%
>
> B. 25%
>
> C. 50%
>
> D. 65%

Here's How to Crack It

The question asks for a percent increase, so we need to use the percent change formula. Your equation should look like this:

It can often be confusing to determine which of the numbers is the "original amount." In this case, the original amount is the number from 1998. Now reduce the fraction to $\frac{1}{4}$, which translates to 25%. B is the correct answer.

Notice that 20% is also an answer choice. If you incorrectly made 50,000 the original amount, you would have gotten 20% as the correct answer. Be careful on these questions—test writers will always include answer choices designed to trap you.

CHAPTER SUMMARY

Use this summary to make sure that you're familiar with the following material:

1. Variables can be used to provide an abstract way of representing a mathematical expression. This is the basis for a specific area of mathematics, known as algebra.

2. Variables can be manipulated in many of the same ways that we manipulate numbers. Most algebraic rules are extensions of the basic rules of mathematics.

3. Simplify algebraic expressions using the same methods that you would use to reduce numbers, such as fractions.

4. Be familiar with how to translate word problem phrases into algebraic expressions. These are the building blocks to creating equations.

5. Be completely familiar with the material presented in the "math flashbacks" section. If you have not mastered this material, you will struggle through the chapters ahead.

ALGEBRAIC EQUATIONS

OVERVIEW

Now that we've discussed variables and algebraic expressions, we'll show you the many ways of solving algebraic equations. Further, we will address special types of equations, such as ratios, proportions, and percent questions. Finally, we will discuss inequalities, which have many of the same properties as equations.

SOLVING AN EQUATION

In the last chapter, we said that an equation is a statement that equates two values—the value on the left side of the equation equals the value on the right side of the equation. An equation might look something like this:

$$3x + 18 = 24$$

And on the Algebra GSE, a sample question might look something like this:

If $3x + 18 = 24$, what is the value of x?

A. 2

B. 6

C. 14

D. 15

Here's How to Crack It

Given the four answer choices, we could figure out the value of x by evaluating the equation, substituting in each of the four answer choices, in this way:

Does 3(2) + 18 = 24? Yes.

Does 3(6) + 18 = 24? No.

Does 3(14) + 18 = 24? No.

Does 3(15) + 18 = 24? No.

See, we tried each expression to see which one gave us a true equality. While this method works with questions that have answer choices, this can't be the only method used to solve for a variable! What if a question doesn't have answer choices, or what if the process is taking too long?

Well, take a look at the question in the problem above. It could be asked many ways: "what is the value of x"; "solve for x"; "x equals?" But, no matter how the GSE authors phrase this question, you have to do one thing when solving algebraic equations—isolate the variable x from all the other numbers. This means getting the variable alone, on one side of the equation, and all the numbers on the other side. To do this, you need to know the GOLDEN RULE OF EQUATIONS: *Whatever you do to the left side of the equation, you must do to the right side of the equation.*

Let's take a look at the equation above.

Well, the variable is on the left side of the equation, so we need to get all the other stuff to the right side of the equation. The first step is to move any lone numbers, in this case, the 18.

$$
\begin{aligned}
3x + 18 &= 24 \\
-18 \quad &-18 \\
\hline
3x - 0 &= 6
\end{aligned}
$$

To make the 18 disappear, we needed to subtract 18 from the left side of the equation. But this means we also need to subtract 18 from the right side of the equation. After simplifying each side of the equation, you can see that there is no longer a value on the left side of the equation. Our new equation is:

$$3x = 6$$

Next, we need to move the number 3 away from the variable x. Currently, 3 and x are multiplied together, so to eliminate the 3 from the left side of the equation, we need to divide $3x$ by 3. Following the golden rule, we also must divide the right side of the equation by 3.

$$\frac{3x}{3} = \frac{6}{3}$$
$$x = 2$$

The 3s cancel each other out on the left side of the equation; we are now left with the value x. Our final equation is $x = 2$, and answer choice A is correct.

Occasionally, you will be presented with a single equation that has more than one variable. Don't worry. The GSE writers will give you a value to enter into the equation.

If $4a + 2b = 32 - a + b$, find the value of a
when $b = 12$.

A. 2

B. 4

C. 6

D. 10

Here's How to Crack It

This problem asks you to do two things. First you need to evaluate the expression with $b = 12$, and next you need to solve for the value of a using the Golden Rule of Equations. Start this problem by rewriting the equation, substituting the number 12 wherever you see b:

$$4a + 2(12) = 32 - a + (12)$$

Next, using the order of operations (PEMDAS), simplify the equation:

$$4a + 24 = 32 - a + 12$$

$$4a + 24 = 44 - a$$

Now you can solve this equation using the techniques we described in the previous example. Isolate the variable a from all other numbers. In this case, both the left side and the right side of the equation contain a. While you figure out on which side of the equation to isolate the variable, keep in mind that it is usually easier to move the smaller value. In this example, we'll move the $-a$ to the left side of the equation:

$$
\begin{array}{rcl}
4a + 24 &=& 44 - a \\
+a & & +a \\
\hline
5a & = & 44
\end{array}
$$

Next, move the 24 to the right side of the equation:

$$5a = 44 - 24$$

$$5a = 20$$

Finally, make the 5 disappear from the left side of the equation by dividing:

$$\frac{5a}{5} = \frac{20}{5}$$

$$a = 4$$

B is the correct answer.

If you see a question that contains an equation that has more than one variable in it, the GSE authors will need to give you additional information to solve that equation. Most often, they will give you the value of one of the variables and ask you to find the other. In future chapters, we will talk about how to solve a series of simultaneous equations (these will involve multiple variables). Here are some additional equations that you can practice manipulating and solving.

Equation Drill
(Answer key can be found on page 66)

1. If $6y - 3 = -9$, then y equals

   A. -2

   B. -1

   C. 1

   D. 2

2. If $n + 2b + p = h - r$, what is the value of h when $n = 8$, $b = \frac{1}{2}$, $p = \frac{3}{4}$, and $r = 6$?

   A. $9\frac{3}{4}$

   B. 15

   C. $15\frac{1}{2}$

   D. $15\frac{3}{4}$

3. If $8c - 12 = 12$, what is twice the value of c?

   A. 0

   B. 3

   C. 6

   D. 32

4. If $3z = 10$, what is the value of $9z$?

   A. 6

   B. 10

   C. 16

   D. 30

Equations That Have Variables on Both Sides

In the problems above, we have solved equations in which the variable appeared on only one side of the equation. Let's solve an equation that has variables on both sides of its equals sign. Let's also make it a little more complex (so you have to use the order of operations to solve the problem):

If $4(n - 2) + 5 = 6n - 5$, then what is the value of n?

   A. -2

   B. -1

   C. 1

   D. 2

Here's How to Crack It

The first step is to expand the left side of the equation and perform all calculations in the parenthesis:

$$4n - 8 + 5 = 6n - 5$$

Now we can simplify the numbers on the left side of the equation:

$$4n - 3 = 6n - 5$$

Next we need to figure out how to isolate n from the rest of the equation. Let's get all values of n on one side of the equation. We could subtract $4n$ from both sides of the equation, or we could subtract $6n$ from both sides of the equation. Does it matter which one we select? No. All that matters is that you use the Golden Rule of Equations, making sure that whatever you do to one side of the equation, you do to the other. Because it is usually easier to deal with a positive number, we will subtract the smaller amount, $4n$, from both sides of the equation:

$$4n - 3 = 6n - 5$$
$$\underline{-4n \qquad -4n}$$
$$-3 = 2n - 5$$

Next move the 5 over to the left side of the equation:

$$-3 = 2n - 5$$
$$\underline{+5 \qquad +5}$$
$$2 = 2n$$

Finally, solve for n by dividing by 2:

$$1 = n$$

The correct answer is C.

Equations with Fractions

Often, an equation that contains fractions can be solved easily by multiplying the entire equation by a denominator that's common to all of its fractions. For example:

If $\dfrac{2}{3}x + \dfrac{1}{2}x = \dfrac{5}{6} + 2x$, then what is the value of x?

A. -1

B. 0

C. $\dfrac{1}{2}$

D. 1

Here's How to Crack It

Look for the common denominator of all of the fractions in the equation. That denominator is 6. Now multiply the entire equation by 6 to remove all fractions:

$$\frac{2}{3}x + \frac{1}{2}x = \frac{5}{6} + 2x$$

$$6\left(\frac{2}{3}x + \frac{1}{2}x\right) = 6\left(\frac{5}{6} + 2x\right)$$

Now, multiply each term using the distributive property that we discussed in the first chapter:

$$6\left(\frac{2}{3}x\right) + 6\left(\frac{1}{2}x\right) = 6\left(\frac{5}{6}\right) + 6(2x)$$

$$4x + 3x = 5 + 12x$$

Now that we have removed all the fractions from the equation, we can isolate the variable and solve for x:

$$
\begin{array}{rcl}
7x & = & 5 + 12x \\
-7x & & -7x \\
\hline
0 & = & 5 + 5x \\
-5 & = & 5x
\end{array}
$$

Dividing by 5 gives us:

$$-1 = x$$

Answer choice A is correct.

Equations That Contain Absolute Values

Remember that the absolute value of a number is defined as its distance from zero on a number line. Therefore, absolute value will either be zero or a positive number. Here is an example of an algebraic equation that uses absolute value:

If $|b| + 4 = 9$, what is the value of b?

Here's How to Crack It

To solve this equation, start, as always, by isolating the variable on one side:

$$
\begin{array}{rcl}
|b| + 4 & = & 9 \\
-4 & & -4 \\
\hline
|b| & = & 5
\end{array}
$$

Since the absolute value of $b = 5$, we have two options for b. The value of b could be either -5 or 5. You can substitute these two values back into the equation to see that each one is a possible solution. When there is more than one possible solution to an equation, you can write:

$$b = 5 \text{ or } b = -5$$

Another shorthand way to write this solution is:

$$b = \{-5, 5\}$$

SPECIFIC EQUATIONS

A number of different mathematical terms and formulas use algebraic equations. In the pages ahead, we will discuss averages, ratios, and proportions, and delve deeper into percent questions. We'll show you the algebraic methods used to solve these problems. We'll even teach you some tricks and strategies so that you may not even have to use algebra on these problems!

Averages

There are a number of ways to describe an average—the GSE writers may use the terms average, arithmetic mean, or mean, but they all describe the same thing. An **average** is defined in this way: In a set of n numbers, the average is the total of the numbers, divided by n. In algebraic form, if we were asked to find the average for four numbers, we could use the following equation:

$$A = \frac{a + b + c + \partial}{4}$$

This equation says that the average is the sum of each number, divided by the number of numbers. Let's make that a little easier. There are three parts to the average equation: the total, the number of things, and the average. Now take a look at the average circle:

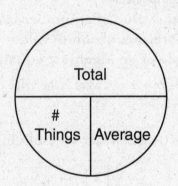

When you get an average question, draw this. You will be given two pieces of information—your job is to find the third.

Example #1: You take three tests and receive grades of 90, 80, and 82. What is your average score?

Solution: Fill in what you know. The total, or sum of the grades, is 252. The number of things is 3. To find the average, divide the total by the number of things. $\frac{252}{3}$ is 84.

Example #2: You score an average of 84 on five tests. What is the total of all five tests?

Solution: You can fill in the average (84), and the number of things (5). To find the total, multiply the two numbers together. 84 × 5, or 420.

Example #3: You score an average of 74 in your history class, and have a total of 296 points. How many tests did you take?

Solution: Here, we know the total (296) and the average (74). To find the number of things, divide the total by the average. $\frac{252}{3}$ or 4, is the answer.

Some average questions will require more than one step, or will ask for information that won't be contained in the average circle. Regardless, always start by finding the third piece of your average circle. Here is a more challenging average question:

If Paula-Ann scored an average of 86 on her first five tests, what is the minimum she must score on her sixth test in order to have an overall average of 88?

A. 84

B. 88

C. 90

D. 98

Here's How to Crack It

Fill out the average circle first. You have the average and the number of things, so we need to find the total. Multiplying 5 by 86 gives us 430. Next let's fill in another average circle with the information we want in the second part of the question. There are six things, and we want an average of 88. The total here is 528. The difference between the totals on the first five tests and all six tests is 98 (528 − 430). D is the correct answer.

Take all average problems one step at a time, and always fill out the average circle.

Ratios

A **ratio** is a comparison. At first, it may seem that ratios are just like fractions, but whereas a fraction compares part of something to a whole, a ratio compares part of something to another part. Ratios can be written in three formats. The ratio of a to b can be written as:

$$\frac{a}{b}$$

The ratio of *a* to *b*

a:b

To understand the difference between ratios and fractions, let's work with the following example: In a 3rd grade class, the ratio of boys to girls is 5:4.

The ratio of boys to girls can be written as: 5/4 or 5:4. Ratios, like fractions, can also be reduced. This ratio does not tell us how many students, total, are in the class; it merely tells us that for every five boys, there are four girls. Be careful with the order of ratios; a ratio of 5:4 is different from a ratio of 4:5.

What is the fractional amount of boys in the class? To find a fraction, we are looking for the part over the whole. Say there are 20 boys in the class, and a whole, or total, of 36 students. The fractional amount of boys is $\frac{20}{36}$ which may be reduced to $\frac{5}{9}$.

 The Ratio Box

If we know that a class has a ratio of boys to girls of 2:1, do we know how many people are in the class? Nope. There could be 20 and 10, or a really large class of 200 boys and 100 girls. The ratio alone does not tell us the actual number of students. We need more information. If we were also told that the class had a total of 90 students, we could find the number of boys and girls in the class. How? By using the Ratio Box, which is shown below:

	Boys	**Girls**	**Whole**
Ratio (parts)	2	1	3
Multiply By			
Actual Number			90

If we treat the initial ratio as "parts," we could find a theoretical "whole." In this example, we know the class is composed of 2 parts boys and 1 part girls, for a total of 3 parts, so we fill in the whole number as 3.

Our next step is to determine how we can make the jump from 3 parts to the whole class of 90 students. To do this, we need to find out what number we need to multiply by 3 in order to get 90. The answer is 30. So let's fill in every space in the second row with the number 30 (the second row will always contain the same number—you multiply evenly across all parts of the ratio):

	Boys	Girls	Whole
Ratio (parts)	2	1	3
Multiply By	30	30	30
Actual Number			90

Our final step is to determine the actual number of boys and the actual number of girls in the class. We can do that by multiplying the two numbers in the Boys column (2 × 30), and the two numbers in the Girls column (1 × 30). Our completed ratio box can be found below:

	Boys	Girls	Whole
Ratio (parts)	2	1	3
Multiply By	30	30	30
Actual Number	60	30	90

From our work, we have found that in a class of 90 students, with a ratio of 2 boys to 1 girl, there are 60 boys and 30 girls.

Here are a few keys to follow:

1. Always use the ratio box on ratio questions—you will be given an initial ratio, and one "actual number."

2. Start by filling in the initial ratio and the actual number; sum the initial ratio to get the whole number of "parts"; determine the multiply number, and write that number in for every column.

3. Find the actual numbers by multiplying down each column.

The ratio box helps you keep track of all the information you need for any type of ratio question. Practice using the ratio box, and ratios will be a breeze come test day.

Here's another example:

> CORE Education services produces two types of products—notebooks and binders. If CORE has an inventory of notebooks and binders in a 3:2 ratio and a total of 100 products in stock, how many notebooks does CORE have in inventory?
>
> A. 5
>
> B. 30
>
> C. 40
>
> D. 60

After reading the question, here is what the ratio box should look like:

	Notebooks	Binders	Whole
Ratio (parts)	3	2	5
Multiply By			
Actual Number			100

Next, we need to find the multiplier. What do you multiply 5 by in order to get 100? The answer is 20. Here is what the completed ratio box looks like:

	Notebooks	Binders	Whole
Ratio (parts)	3	2	5
Multiply By	20	20	20
Actual Number	60	40	100

The correct answer is D, 60. Be careful not to select 40, which is the total number of binders in inventory.

The ratio box is something you should definitely put it in your bag of tricks.

Proportions

Some GSE questions will define a relationship between two things and ask you to use this relationship to find other proportional values. Let's take a look at a sample proportion question:

If Chris can iron three shirts in 18 minutes, how long will it take him to iron 12 shirts?

A. 1 hour 4 minutes

B. 1 hour 12 minutes

C. 1 hour 18 minutes

D. 1 hour 44 minutes

Here's How to Crack It

Every proportion question will contain two relationships—one that is given to you, and one with a missing piece of information. In this example, we're given the relationship

$$\frac{3 \text{ (shirts)}}{18 \text{ (minutes)}}$$

Set this relationship equal to the proportion we want to find the missing value for:

$$\frac{3 \text{ (shirts)}}{18 \text{ (minutes)}} = \frac{12 \text{ (shirts)}}{x \text{ (minutes)}}$$

In order for a proportion equation to be correct, notice that the units must be in the same order (in this example, both fractions contain shirts in the numerator and minutes in the denominator). Further, the units must always be the same (you couldn't have minutes in one fraction and hours in the other). Now, we can cross multiply to solve the equation:

$$3x = (12)(18)$$

$$x = (4)(18)$$

$$x = 72 \text{ minutes}$$

So it takes Chris 72 minutes to iron 12 shirts. While 72 minutes is not an answer choice, we know that there are 60 minutes in an hour, so 72 minutes equals 1 hour, 12 minutes. B is the correct answer.

Let's try another proportion problem, this time in the form of an algebraic equation:

If $\frac{(2x - 2)}{3} = \frac{(3x - 5)}{6}$ what is the value of x?

A. −3

B. −1

C. 3

D. 6

Here's How to Crack It

The first step to solving this proportion is to cross-multiply, in order to remove the fractions from the equation:

$$(2x - 2)6 = (3x - 5)3$$

$$12x - 12 = 9x - 15$$

At this point, we can solve this equation as usual, isolating x:

$$3x - 12 = -15$$
$$\underline{+12 \quad +12}$$
$$\frac{3x}{3} = \frac{-3}{3}$$
$$x = -1$$

Answer choice B is the correct answer.

Percent Equations

In the last chapter, we discussed the basics of percentages, and ways in which to translate specific percent phrases into mathematical equivalents. For example, 15 percent of 80 can be rewritten as:

$$\left(\frac{15}{100}\right)80$$

This translation of percents can be very helpful in creating algebraic equations. Here is an example:

> At Joe's farm there are 20 cows, 17 pigs, and 13 horses. What percent of the animals on the farm are not pigs?
>
> A. 20%
>
> B. 33%
>
> C. 34%
>
> D. 66%

Here's How to Crack It

Take a look at the question contained in the problem. We can translate this equation to turn this word problem into a specific algebraic equation:

What percent   can be written as $\dfrac{x}{100}$

| *of the animals on the farm* | can be written as | $\times 50$ |
| *are not pigs* | can be written as | $= 33$ |

To summarize, we have the equation $\left(\dfrac{x}{100}\right)50 = 33$

This equation was created simply by translating percent terms into their mathematical equivalents. Now, let's solve for x:

$$\left(\frac{x}{100}\right)50 = 33$$

$$\frac{50x}{100} = 33$$

$$50x = (33)(100)$$

$$50x = 3300$$

$$x = 66$$

Answer choice D is correct.

INEQUALITIES

Up to this point, we have been working with equations that are equalities, meaning that they're related to one another by an equals sign. An **inequality** is another way of describing a relationship between two different numbers or expressions. You encounter many inequalities in your daily life, some examples might be:

- *There must be a minimum of nine players on a baseball team.*

- *You must take more than three classes during your senior year, but you cannot take more than seven classes.*

- *The school will put on a play if more than 18 people are interested in participating in it.*

Inequality Symbols

Let's review the four symbols that you need to be familiar with when dealing with inequalities.

>	greater than	$7 > 2$	7 is greater than 2
<	less than	$2 < 7$	2 is a number less than 7
≥	greater than or equal to	$x \geq 5$	x is greater than or equal to 5
≤	less than or equal to	$5 \leq x$	5 is less than or equal to x

Any math statement that includes one of these four symbols is an inequality. You probably learned about these signs way back in elementary school. You might have been taught that the inequality sign was an alligator, which points to the larger number because it is hungry and it wants to eat the larger number! But don't worry about the alligator, just make sure you know the differences between these signs.

Using these symbols, we can translate the sentences above into inequality statements:

- *There must be a minimum of 9 players on a baseball team* could be represented by $p \geq 9$.

- *You must take more than three classes during your senior year, but you cannot take more than seven classes* could be denoted by $c > 3$ and $c \leq 7$, which can be summarized by the following inequality: $3 < c \leq 7$.

- *The school will put on a play if more than 18 people are interested in participating in it* could be expressed by the inequality $p > 18$.

Solving Inequalities

If $3x + 18 > 24$, which of the following expressions gives all the possible values of x?

A. $x > 2$

B. $x < 6$

C. $x > 14$

D. $x < 15$

Here's How to Crack It

When solving an inequality, treat the inequality sign just like an equals sign, and remember to use the golden rule of equations (whatever you do to one side, you must do the other side).

$$3x + 18 > 24$$
$$\underline{-18 \quad -18}$$
$$3x \qquad > \quad 6$$

$$\frac{3x}{3} > \frac{6}{3}$$

$$x > 2$$

Answer choice A is correct.

As you can see, in some ways inequalities are just like equations. Make sure you isolate the variable, and be sure to treat both sides of the inequality equally. But when you're dealing with inequalities, there is one important exception: **If** *you are multiplying or dividing by a negative number in an equality, you must flip the sign of the inequality!*

Here is an example:

> If $-7a + 3 < 24$, then which of the following expressions gives all the possible values of a?
>
> A. $a = 3$
>
> B. $a < -3$
>
> C. $a > -3$
>
> D. $a > 6$

Here's How to Crack It

As you would with any inequality or equation, try to isolate the variable on one side of the equation. In this case, start by moving the 3 to the other side of the equation; this leaves us with the inequality

$$-7a < 21$$

At this point, we need to divide by -7 in order to isolate the variable:

$$\frac{-7a}{-7} < \frac{21}{-7}$$

This means that we need to divide by a negative number, so we must flip the inequality, then proceed with the division as usual:

$$a > -3$$

Answer choice C is the correct answer. Be careful when selecting your answer choice! The GSE writers will almost always include an answer choice that looks correct, except that the inequality sign is pointing in the wrong direction.

Inequality Drill

(Answer key can be found on page 66)

1. If $-3x + 6 \geq 18$, which of the following must be true?

    A. $x \leq -4$

    B. $x \leq 6$

    C. $x \geq -4$

    D. $x \geq -6$

2. If $5x + 3 < 28$, then which of the following expressions gives all the possible values of x?

    A. $x < 5$

    B. $x < -5$

    C. $x > 0$

    D. $x > 5$

3. If $-5x - 21 < 14$, which of the following must be true?

    A. $x > 7$

    B. $x > -7$

    C. $x < 7$

    D. $x < -7$

WORD PROBLEM STRATEGIES

Throughout this chapter, we have discussed the different types of questions you may be asked on the Algebra GSE. For each type of question, we have discussed the type of equation that you will need to construct. Now we'll show you something else that you can put in your bag of tricks. On some multiple-choice questions, you may not have to use an equation at all. Instead, let the answer choices do the work for you! This important technique is called Backsolving.

 **Backsolving**

Let's take a look at a typical algebra word problem:

> Marcello has 34 more dimes than nickels. If he owns a total of 76 coins, how many nickels does Marcello own?
>
> A. 21 nickels
>
> B. 40 nickels
>
> C. 42 nickels
>
> D. 110 nickels

The traditional way to solve this problem is to set up a system of equations. You could assign a variable for dimes, another variable for nickels, and a third one for coins. In this particular question, traditional algebra would take a while. In fact, you would need to create two equations, each with two variables.

The problem asks us for the number of nickels that Marcello owns, and presents us with four possible answer choices. If we were to set up the equations properly, we'd find one of those four answer choices.

Isn't there a better way?! What if we use those answer choices to our advantage? It has to be one of the four, right? Rather than try to create our own equations, we might as well try plugging in one of the answer choices into the problem, and see if it works. If not, let's keep trying until we find the answer choice that does.

As we mentioned, this technique is called Backsolving. Whenever you are presented with an algebra question, in which there are numbers in the answer choices, start plugging in the answer choices to see which is correct. You may find that backsolving is easier, more accurate, and more efficient than creating an equation (or a system of equations).

Let's solve the sample problem above, using Backsolving. Start with answer choice C, 42 nickels (we'll explain why we started with C in a minute). Let's see if we can work back through the problem as though Marcello owned 42 nickels.

The first statement tells us that Marcello has 34 more dimes than nickels. If Marcello owns 42 nickels, then he owns 76 dimes, for a total of 118 coins. The problem indicates that Marcello owns a total of 76 coins, so is C the correct answer? Nope! Using the value of 42 nickels, the problem did not work correctly, so we can eliminate answer choice C.

If you take a look at the answer choices, you can see that they are in order, from smallest to largest. In general, the answer choices on the Algebra GSE will be in ascending or descending order. We started with C, one of the middle values, and in the example above, we showed that C is not correct. Can you tell if we'll need a larger number or a smaller number? Sure! When we plugged in the value of 42 nickels, we found that the total number of coins was much larger than we wanted. Therefore, the correct answer will be fewer than 42 nickels. In this case, we can eliminate answer choice D (it will provide an even larger total), and move to the next smaller answer choice, B.

Answer choice B tells us that Marcello has a total of 40 nickels. If this were the case, this would mean that he owns 74 dimes. This gives him a total of 114 coins—again, a number that's much larger than the one we're looking for. Eliminate answer choice B.

There's only one answer choice left that makes sense! At this point, feel free to select answer choice A, without doing the math (for purposes of this example, we'll finish the work). Answer choice A says that there are 21 nickels. If Marcello owns 21 nickels, then he must have 55 dimes. This gives us a total of 76 coins—exactly what we're looking for! Answer choice A is correct.

Let's take a minute to summarize what we just did. First we identified a specific type of algebra word problem—its answer choices were numbers. Because there are numbers in the answer choices, we plug these numbers back into the problem to see which one works. In order to be most efficient, we started with one of the middle values. This helped us estimate which way to go if the middle answer choice was incorrect. Once we identified the correct way to go (up or down the answer choices), be sure to eliminate any impossible ones.

Backsolving turns difficult algebra questions into arithmetic problems. Rather than worrying about creating complicated equations, focus on using the answer choices to your advantage.

We'll do two more typical Backsolving questions to be sure you're familiar with this technique:

> Adam is half as old as Bob and three times
> as old as Cindy. If the sum of their ages is
> 40, what is Bob's age?
>
> A. 3
>
> B. 12
>
> C. 18
>
> D. 24

Here's How to Crack It

We have an algebra question that has numbers as its answer choices, so Backsolve! The answer choices tell us Bob's age. Try starting with Bob's age at 12 (answer choice B). If Bob is 12, then Adam is 6 and Cindy is 2. The sum of their ages is 20. We're looking for a choice that makes the sum of their ages 40, so eliminate B.

Now, which way should we go? Should we increase Bob's age to 18 (answer choice C) or decrease his age to 3 (answer choice A)? When we tried Bob at age 12, the sum of their ages was much smaller than we wanted. Therefore, we should increase Bob's age to 18, and try answer choice C. Before trying answer choice C, eliminate answer choice A—which is clearly incorrect.

If Bob is 18, then Adam is half his age, or 9. Cindy is a third of Adam's age, so she is 3. If we sum their ages, we get 18 + 9 + 3 = 30. The problem indicates that the sum of their ages is 40, so answer choice C is not correct. Eliminate it.

We're left with only one answer choice, so D must be the correct answer. Want to see the work? If Bob is 24, then Adam is half his age, or 12. Cindy is a third of Adam's age, so she is 4. The sum of their ages, 24 + 12 + 4, equals 40. We have solved the problem.

> If there are four times as many women as men employed by the Acme Insurance Company, then how many of the 75 workers are women?
>
> A. 90
>
> B. 60
>
> C. 45
>
> D. 15

Here's How to Crack It

Did you recognize it as a Backsolving problem? It might have looked like a ratio box problem to you at first, but we have a statement for which an algebraic equation could be written, and we also have numbers in the answer choices. But before you even start Backsolving, you could use another great math technique, Ballparking. The question tells us that there are a total of 75 workers. Thus, answer choice A doesn't make sense. The number of women in the company can't be greater than the total number of employees! Eliminate A.

In general, we have always said to start with a middle answer choice. In this case, since we have eliminated answer choice A, start with the middle remaining value, which is C. Answer choice C tells us that there are 45 women in the work force. If there are 45 women, and a total of 75 employees, then there must be 30 men (75 – 45). Are there four times as many women as men, meaning is 4(30) = 45? No, so we can eliminate choice C.

There needs to be a greater number of women in order to meet the ratio, so let's move to answer choice B. At this point, using POE we already know that B is correct, but let's do the math. Answer choice B tells us that there are 60 women in the work force. If there are 60 women and a total of 75 employees, then there must be 15 men (75 – 60). Are there four times as many women as men? Yes. 60 is four times greater than 15 (if you aren't sure, simply reduce the fraction). $\frac{60}{15} = \frac{12}{3} = \frac{4}{1}$. Answer choice B is correct.

Will Backsolving Work for Every Question?

Unfortunately, no. Many questions on the GSE will have to be solved by manipulating the information that is given to you. Ballparking is just one of a number of techniques you can throw into your bag of tricks. Remember the keys to identifying a Backsolving question:

- Numbers in the answer choices

- Does it seem like an algebra question? That is, do you feel like you need to start writing an algebraic equation in order to solve the problem? If so, you've probably identified a Backsolving question.

- The question asks for a specific amount — Backsolving questions will typically end in concrete statements, such as "what is the value of x"; "how many tools does Bill have"; or "how many tickets were purchased."

DRILL ANSWER KEY

Equation Drill (page 48)	Inequality Drill (page 62)
1. B	1. A
2. D	2. A
3. C	3. B
4. D	

CHAPTER SUMMARY

You should now be familiar and comfortable with the following items:

1. The Golden Rule of Equations is essential to solving equations and inequalities. Whatever you do to one side of the equation, you must do to the other side of the equation.

2. Isolate a variable from all other numbers in order to solve an equation.

3. A useful trick to get rid of fractions is to multiply both sides of an equation by the lowest common denominator of all fractions in the equation.

4. Averages define the total sum of a group of things divided by the number of things. To set up average equations, use the average circle.

5. Ratios define a relationship between one part of a group to another part of a group. Equations in ratio questions can be created by using the ratio box.

6. Remember that ratios compare a part to a part, whereas fractions compare a part to a whole.

7. Proportions project a relationship from one scale to another. Equations can be solved by cross-multiplying the proportions.

8. Percent equations can be created by translating questions into their mathematical equivalents.

9. Inequalities are just like equations, with one notable exception: when multiplying or dividing by a negative number, flip the direction of the inequality.

10. Backsolving is a great tool to use in solving some multiple-choice questions. Just plug the numbers from the answer choices into the word problem, starting with the middle choices. This tool is also helpful for other algebra problems.

11. The Bowtie can be used to quickly add, subtract, or compare fractions.

12. Always check the answer choices to a problem before solving it. You may find that you can eliminate answer choices that do not fit the question.

FACTORING POLYNOMIALS

OVERVIEW

This chapter reviews polynomials, including factoring of polynomials, and solutions to systems of equations. A **polynomial** is a mathematical expression that has more than one term in it. A **monomial** is an expression that is a number, a variable, or a product of numbers and variables. The phrase polynomial covers all expressions of more than one term. Don't worry about separating out polynomials into more specific terms like binomials, or trinomials; again, definitions will not appear on the Algebra GSE.

In this chapter, we are going to begin by reviewing how to combine monomials and polynomials. We will then discuss how these expressions can be factored, manipulated, and reduced. The factoring methods you'll learn here are crucial to solving many different types of algebra questions.

Finally, in this chapter, we are going to review how to deal with a system of equations. That is, how do you work with more than one equation at a time? Well, in this chapter, we'll tell you.

COMBINING MONOMIALS

As a quick review, let's make sure that you are comfortable combining terms. For example:

What is $(4x^5y^5)(-2x^6y^4)$?

Here's How to Crack It

This is a multiplication problem. You don't need to multiply in any specific order; however, you will want to combine all like terms to reduce this expression as much as possible.

If you were to expand this out, you would get:

$$4x^5y^5 \cdot 2x^6y^4$$

$$= (4 \cdot -2)(x^5x^6)(y^5y^4)$$

$$= (-8)(x^{11})(y^9)$$

$$= -8x^{11}y^9$$

In the solution above, we combined like terms and simplified the expression as much as we could.

Here's another example:

Simplify the following expression: $\dfrac{8x^5y^{12}}{-2x^3y^{10}}$

Here's How to Crack It

Remember to divide like things (coefficients with coefficients, etc):

$$8 \div -2 = -4$$
$$x^5 \div x^3 = x^2$$
$$y^{12} \div y^{10} = y^2$$

The solution is $-4x^2y^2$.

POLYNOMIALS

As we mentioned in the overview, a polynomial is a mathematical expression that involves more than one term. Some examples of polynomials are:

$$5z - 2 \qquad 3x^2 + 2x - 5 \qquad 4xy + 4 - y$$

A polynomial is created when two or more monomials are put together, usually through addition or subtraction. Let's take a close look at one polynomial to make sure you are familiar with some vocabulary words commonly used with them:

$$3x^2 + 2x - 5$$

A **coefficient** is defined as the number associated with and preceding the variable in an expression. In the equation above, there are two coefficients: 3 and 2. When a number is present in a term, unassociated with a variable, it is referred to as a **constant**. -5 is a constant in the equation above. A polynomial can also be described by the number of degrees it has. The degree of a term is the sum of the exponents of the variables. For example, the degree of $3x^2 = 2$. The degree of $2x$ is 1 (x is raised to the first power). The degree of -5 is 0 (there are no variables nor exponents in this term). The degree of a polynomial is simply the highest degree of its terms. For the polynomial above, the degree is 2 (because its highest polynomial term is 2).

As a general rule, it is easiest to work with polynomials when they are arranged in descending order with regard to degree of term. If given a set of terms in a polynomial, you should first rearrange the numbers in descending order for variables. This will be useful when we start factoring polynomials. For example, the polynomial $3x^5 + 5x^2 - 2x^8 + 5x - 3 + x^4$ should be rearranged in the following format:

$$-2x^8 + 3x^5 + x^4 + 5x^2 + 5x - 3$$

This format will help you quickly solve various problems and equations.

Adding Polynomials

The process of adding polynomials is very similar to adding variables. In order to combine terms, they must have the same variable and the same degree of variable. For example, you know that $x^2 + 2x^2 = 3x^2$. How about the following: Can you add together $3x^3 + 2x^2$? No, it does *not* equal $5x^5$. The variables are not raised to the same power, and therefore cannot be combined.

Consider the following example:

What is $(-5m^2 - 2m - 2m^3 - 4) +$
$(m^4 - 6m^2 + 7m - 10)$?

Here's How to Crack It

When adding a pair of polynomials, perform the following steps:

1. Order each polynomial in descending order for a particular variable.

2. Put like terms together in a column format.

3. Add each column together.

Using the steps above, here's the solution:

$$
\begin{array}{r}
m^4 \qquad\ - 6m^2 + 7m - 10 \\
+ \quad - 2m^3 - 5m^2 - 2m - 4 \\
\hline
m^4 - 2m^3 - 11m^2 + 5m - 14
\end{array}
$$

So, the correct answer is $m^4 - 2m^3 - 11m^2 + 5m - 14$.

Subtracting Polynomials

Subtracting polynomials works in a way that's similar to the method we used above. When you subtract a polynomial, you must subtract the entire second polynomial from the first polynomial. Remember that subtracting a number is the same thing as adding its additive inverse. For example, $5 - 2$ is the same expression as $5 + (-2)$.

Use this rule to help make sure you subtract polynomials correctly. Here's an example:

What is $(m^4 - 6m^2 + 7m - 10) - (-5m^2 - 2m - 2m^3 - 4)$?

Here's How to Crack It:

When subtracting a pair of polynomials, perform the following steps:

1. Order each polynomial in descending order of degree of its terms.

2. Put like terms together in a column format.

3. Subtract the second value from the first value in each column.

Using the steps above, here's the solution:

$$m^4 \qquad - 6m^2 + 7m - 10$$
$$- \quad \underline{\quad -2m^3 - 5m^2 - 2m - 4 \quad}$$

Subtracting requires that we add the additive inverse for each term in the second polynomial. To put it an easier way, the sign changes for every value in the second polynomial. Therefore:

$$m^4 \qquad -6m^2 + 7m - 10$$
$$+ \quad \underline{\quad 2m^3 + 5m^2 + 2m + 4 \quad}$$
$$m^4 \quad 2m^3 \quad - m^2 \qquad 9m - 6$$

So the correct answer is $m^4 + 2m^3 - m^2 + (-m^2) - 6$.

Notice how each value went from a negative to a positive when we subtracted the second polynomial.

Multiplying Polynomials

We have used the distributive property to multiply a set of numbers together, and we can use this property again to multiply polynomials. Consider the following example:

Multiply the following polynomials together:
$(x^2 + 3)(x^3 + 2x + 4)$

Here's How to Crack It

You can use the distributive property to multiply the two polynomials together:

$$x^2(x^3 + 2x + 4) + 3(x^3 + 2x + 4) =$$

$$x^5 + 2x^3 + 4x^2 + 3x^3 + 6x + 12 =$$

$$x^5 + 5x^3 + 4x^2 + 6x + 12$$

Another method to use when multiplying polynomials is to multiply in columns. We did something similar to this when we added and subtracted polynomials. Start by multiplying each term at the top by every term at the bottom. Use columns to align like terms. Then, add together to summarize the equation. Using the example we just saw:

$$(x^2 + 3)$$
$$\underline{(x^3 + 2x + 4)}$$
$$x^5 \qquad\qquad + 3x^3$$

(here, we multiplied the bottom term x^3 by every term on the top. We left a space between the two terms in case we get a number that is in the x^4 power). Let's continue with the second part of the multiplication:

$$+ \qquad 2x^3 + \qquad 6x$$
$$+ \qquad\underline{\qquad 4x^2 \qquad + 12}$$
$$x^5 + 5x^3 + 4x^2 + 6x + 12$$

FACTORING

Factoring is pretty much the reverse of multiplying. Remember when we defined factors, in chapter 3? As in, the factors of 24 are 1, 2, 3, 4, 6, 8, 12, 24. When a number is factored, it is broken down into two smaller numbers. This is also true when you factor algebraic expressions—in factoring algebraic expressions, larger expressions are broken down into two or more expressions.

Let's start by factoring a simple term (a monomial). If you were asked to factor the term $24x^2$, there would be a number of different ways to do so. A few of these ways are shown below:

$$= (x)(24x) \qquad\qquad = (2x)(12x) \qquad\qquad = (3x)(8x)$$
$$= (4x)(6x) \qquad\qquad = (2)(12x^2) \qquad\qquad = (4)(6x^2)$$

As you can see, sometimes there are many different ways to factor a single term. To make sure your factorization is correct, simply multiply the terms back together, and see if you end up with the original expression.

You will need to use factoring most often when you have multiple terms. Let's start with the following example:

$$6xy^2 + 9y$$

In order to factor this expression, your first challenge is to find a common factor within each term. To translate, is there a number or variable that you could factor out of each expression? In the example above, there are two terms that are common factors; 3 and y. Factored out, they look like this:

$$3y(2xy) + 3y(3)$$

Note that our expression is still intact. We haven't changed the value of the expression; only the way in which it is written. Now that we have removed common factors from each term, we can simplify this expression using the distributive property:

$$3y(2xy) + 3y(3)$$

is the same as:

$$3y(2xy + 3)$$

Multiply again if you want, to make sure that the expression above correctly and completely factors the expression $6xy^2 + 9y$.

Let's do one more example:

Factor the polynomial $5x^3 + 5$

Here's How to Crack It
So your first challenge in a factoring question is to find common factors within each term. In the example above, we can factor a 5 from each term, as shown below:

$$5(x^3) + 5(1)$$

Now simplify to get:

$$5(x^3 + 1)$$

Note: Remember, if you completely factor an expression (like you did with the coefficient 5 in the example above), you will still have a value of 1 left over in your polynomial.

Factoring Polynomials
Before we talk more about factoring, let's go back to multiplying. Can you multiply the following expression?

$$(x + 3)(x + 4)$$

You should be able to. To do so, simply use the distributive property:

$$= x(x + 4) + 3(x + 4)$$

$$= x^2 + 4x + 3x + 12$$

$$= x^2 + 7x + 12$$

Great. Now, since multiplying these expressions is so easy (but you'll find you have to do it pretty often), you may want to learn a shorthand method of multiplying such terms together. This is known as the **FOIL** method. FOIL stands for "First, Outer, Inner, Last." This acronym gives you a tool to remind you of all the single multiplications you need to do when multiplying two polynomials. Let's do the above example again, this time using the FOIL method:

$$(x + 3)(x + 4) =$$

$$\textbf{F: } (x)(x)$$

$$\textbf{O: } (x)(4)$$

$$\textbf{I: } (3)(x)$$

$$\textbf{L: } (3)(4)$$

$$= x^2 + 4x + 3x + 12$$

$$= x^2 + 7x + 12$$

The FOIL method helps you perform these calculations as quickly as possible.

Now, let's try the reverse. What if we asked you to factor the following polynomial:

$$x^2 + 7x + 12$$

How would you do this? You know the correct answer, because we started with it, to get to the solution in the problem above. But in order to factor this expression, think of the FOIL method, but this time, working backwards. How do we get the term x^2? By multiplying $x \cdot x$, and already we know the first's, or the beginnings of our factored expression:

$$(x \quad)(x \quad)$$

Next, look at other two numbers. The coefficient of 12 tells us that the product of two numbers will be 12. This information is not enough. There are many combinations that will produce the value of 12:

$$1, 12 \qquad 2, 6 \qquad 3, 4 \qquad -1, -12 \qquad -2, -6, \text{ etc.}$$

But using the middle term can help us solve this part. The middle term, $7x$, tells us that the sum of the two numbers will be a $+7$. What two numbers have a product of $+12$ and a sum of $+7$? Looking at our list of possible factors of 12, you can see that 3, 4 is the correct pair. We can insert this into our factored expression, making it:

$$(x + 4)(x + 3)$$

Let's try one more example that uses positive terms:

$$\text{Factor } y^2 + 12y + 35$$

Here's How to Crack It

We are going to use the FOIL method in reverse. To get the value of y^2, our only option is to multiply $y \cdot y$:

$$(y \quad)(y \quad)$$

Next, how do we get the value of 35? Some options are 1, 35 and 5, 7. What two numbers produce a sum of 12 and a product of 35? 5 and 7.

$$(y + 5)(y + 7)$$

Not all of the polynomials you'll need to factor will contain only positive terms, however. Here's an example of one that contains both positive and negative terms:

$$\text{Factor } y^2 - 4y - 12$$

Here's How to Crack It

The first part of this factoring is exactly like our previous expressions:

$$(y \quad)(y \quad)$$

Next we see that the product of two coefficients is -12. How can we get to a value of -12? There are many ways:

$$-1, 12 \qquad -12, 1 \qquad -2, 6 \qquad -6, 2 \qquad -3, 4 \qquad -4, 3$$

The sum of these two numbers needs to be -4. Therefore, the set of $-6, 2$ is the correct set:

$$(y - 6)(y + 2)$$

Notice that it is very important it is to make sure that the negative sign goes with the correct coefficient. If you place the negative sign on the wrong number, the factored term will be incorrect!

Add This to Your Bag of Tricks!

While you are probably familiar with how to factor polynomials, you should review this chart:

If you have a polynomial in the form of $x^2 + bx + c$:

If the b term is	And if the c term is	Then your solution requires	And...
+	+	2 positive numbers	
−	−	1 positive, 1 negative	larger is negative
+	−	1 positive, 1 negative	larger number is positive
−	+	2 negative numbers	

More Complicated Factoring

What if we added a coefficient in front of the x^2 term in a polynomial? For example, what if you had to factor something like this:

$$6x^2 + 23x + 20$$

Well, with this polynomial, we need to determine how to split up the x value and the coefficient. Start by looking at the signs—both are positive, so we need two positive numbers:

$$1, 20 \quad \text{or} \quad 2, 10 \quad \text{or} \quad 4, 5$$

Next we need to find two values that together will equal $6x^2$:

$$6x, x \quad \text{or} \quad 2x, 3x$$

Finally, we need to combine these values in some sort of way so that we get a value of 23 in the middle. We could consider writing out every possible solution from the numbers given, but there are 12 possible combinations of these numbers.

Because we want to get a combined value of $23x$, the pair 1, 20 will probably not work (it will create a value too high for $23x$). The solution, through trial and error, can be found below:

$$(2x + 5)(3x + 4)$$

A check with the FOIL method indicates that we have:

$$F: 6x^2$$

$$O: 8x$$

$$I: 15x$$

$$L: 20$$

$$= 6x^2 + 23x + 20$$

Is there a magical solution to the more complicated polynomials? Not really. The more you practice factoring, the more you will intuitively get a feel for which combinations of numbers will produce a desired result.

Special Factoring Rules

In your algebra class, you've probably been asked to simplify many different types of algebraic expressions. Some of these expressions will follow specific patterns, and are associated with certain rules. In the pages ahead, we'll tackle some of these special factoring rules.

The Difference of Squares

The phrase difference of squares gives us a big hint about how this specific rule works. Look at the expression below:

$$(x + y)(x - y) = x^2 - y^2$$

There are two reasons why you should be familiar with this equation. First, it will save you time when multiplying some algebraic systems. Instead of using the FOIL method, you can expand anything that's in the $(x + y)(x - y)$ format quickly if you remember this formula. The second reason is that it allows you to factor easily.

In order to use the difference of squares formula, you need to see the following, in an algebraic expression:

1. There need to be two terms.

2. Each term needs to be a square.

3. There must be a minus sign between the terms.

Let's take a look at a few examples of polynomials that can be factored using the difference of squares rule: $x^2 - y^2$

$$9x^2 - 25$$

$$16y^2 - 36$$

$$x^2 - 49$$

To factor these expressions, take the square root of each term. Then add and subtract the two terms. The solutions to the above expressions are written below:

$$= (3x + 5)(3x - 5)$$

$$= (4y^2 + 6)(4y^2 - 6)$$

$$= (x + 7)(x - 7)$$

Here's one more to try:

Factor the expression $81a^6 - 49$

Here's How to Crack It

Are the two terms squares? Yes! The square root of each term is:

$$9a^3 \qquad 7$$

Because the two are perfect squares, we can factor using the difference of squares:

$$(9a^3 + 7)(9a^3 - 7)$$

More Special Factoring Equations

Let's start with the following example:

Factor $x^2 + 6x + 9$

From the methods that we've already have studied, the correct answer is:

$$(x + 3)(x + 3)$$

If you look at this solution, you will notice that the two factored terms are the same. In fact, if we wanted to simplify the above expression further, we could, as follows:

$$(x + 3)^2$$

There are some polynomials that can be simplified as much as the equation above; they're known as **trinomial squares**. But don't worry about the name, just recognize that this is another expression that uses two squares.

 Two More Equations for Your Bag of Tricks:

- If you have a polynomial in the form $x^2 + 2xy + y^2$, you can quickly factor the expression to $(x + y)^2$

- If you have a polynomial in the form $x^2 - 2xy + y^2$, you can quickly factor the expression to $(x - y)^2$

FACTORING TO SOLVE EQUATIONS

Now that you know how to factor algebraic expressions, you can also use factoring to help you solve for a variable. Let's start by working with a simple equation:

$$2x - 3 = 0$$

All we have to do is isolate the variable and solve for x:

$$2x = 3$$

$$x = \frac{3}{2}$$

The process is only slightly more complicated for polynomial expressions. Take the following example:

If $2x^2 + x - 6 = 0$, then solve for x

Here's How to Crack It

At first, you may think that trial and error is one possible method for finding the value of x. You might be tempted to simply plug in some numbers and hope that you will pick a value that gets you the correct answer (in fact, this is often a great strategy to use with multiple-choice questions, as we discussed with Backsolving). But there is another, more straightforward method to find the values of x.

First see if you can factor the expression. You can. The equation now becomes:

$$(2x - 3)(x + 2) = 0$$

Now that you have correctly factored the equation, you can set each term equal to 0. You can do this because of a special property of 0—anything times 0 is 0. Algebra teachers would name this the principle of zero products, but all you need to remember is that you should set each part of the equation equal to 0, and solve:

$$2x - 3 = 0 \qquad \text{and} \qquad x + 2 = 0$$
$$2x = 3 \qquad\qquad\qquad x = -2$$
$$x = 3/2$$

There are two solutions to x: -2, and $\frac{3}{2}$. This is referred to as the solution set for x, or the **roots** of the equation.

See if you can find the roots for x in the following equation: $x^2 + 6x = -8$

Here's How to Crack It

This polynomial is not written in a form that you are used to seeing. In order to get this equation in standard form, rewrite the expression and set it equal to 0:

$$x^2 + 6x + 8 = 0$$

Next, factor the equation:

$$(x + 4)(x + 2) = 0$$

$$x + 4 = 0 \qquad x + 2 = 0$$

$$x = -4 \qquad x = -2$$

The solution set is $x = \{-4, -2\}$

SOLUTIONS TO A SYSTEM

The phrase **system** is used whenever we deal with a set of equations in hopes of finding a common solution. Another common phrase for this situation is "simultaneous equations." We will use the following equations to demonstrate some methods over the next few pages:

$$x + 2y = 7$$

$$x = y + 4$$

Let's consider the second equation: $x = y + 4$. There are many possible solutions to this equation. A few of them are:

$$4, 0 \qquad 3, -1 \qquad 2, -2 \qquad 5, 1 \qquad 6, -2 \qquad 7, -3 \text{ etc.}$$

We don't know which one is correct. In fact, if we were asked to find the solution to this equation alone, we wouldn't be able to do it, because there are an infinite number of solutions. In fact, a general rule for finding solutions to multivariable algebraic expressions is that you need to have an equal number of equations and variables in order to find a solution.

Now which one of the following possible solutions fits into the first equation? Let's try some of the following to see if they work.

(4, 0):
$$x + 2y = 7$$
$$4 + 2(0) = 7$$
$$4 = 7$$

(4, 0) is not a solution.

(2, –2):
$$x + 2y = 7$$
$$2 + 2(-2) = 7$$
$$2 - 4 = 7$$
$$-2 = 7$$

(2, –2) is not a solution.

$$(5, 1): \qquad x + 2y = 7$$

$$(5) + 2(1) = 7$$

$$7 = 7$$

Yes! (5, 1) is a solution of $x + 2y = 7$

Because the solution of $x = 5$ and $y = 1$ is valid for both equations, we can state that (5, 1) is a solution to this system of equations.

You probably don't want to resort to this trial-and-error method of solving a system of equations, so below, we'll go over two alternate ways.

The Substitution Method

You can use the substitution method to quickly solve systems of equations. In this method, you first need to isolate one variable in one equation. Let's go back to our system of examples:

$$x + 2y = 7$$

$$x = y + 4$$

Right now, we already have one equation in which a variable is isolated: the second one. We can take the value of x from the second equation into the first equation:

$$(y + 4) + 2y = 7$$

$$3y + 4 = 7$$

$$3y = 3$$

$$y = 1$$

Now that we have solved for the value of y, substitute this value of y into either equation in order to get the value of x:

$$x = y + 4$$

$$x = (1) + 4$$

$$x = 5$$

So the solution of the system is (5, 1).

Try one more example using the method of substitution:

If $3x + 2y = 10$, and $x + 4y = 20$, find the solution set.

Here's How to Crack It

The first step is to isolate a variable in one of the two equations. Let's try using the second equation:

$$x + 4y = 20$$

$$x = 20 - 4y$$

Now substitute this value for x into the first equation:

$$3x + 2y = 10$$

$$3(20 - 4y) + 2y = 10$$

$$60 - 12y + 2y = 10$$

$$-10y = -50$$

$$y = 5$$

With the value of $y = 5$, substitute the value of y into either equation in order to find the value of x (we'll use the second one).

$$x + 4y = 20$$

$$x + 4(5) = 20$$

$$x + 20 = 20$$

$$x = 0$$

Therefore, the solution set to the system of equations is (0, 5).

Combining a System of Equations (The Elimination Method)

Sometimes you might find that the substitution method either takes too long or is not as easy as other possible solutions. Well, another option for solving systems of equations is to combine the two equations, either through addition, subtraction, and even multiplication. We'll try adding the two equations together first. Here's an example:

What is the value of x if
{$3x + y = 5$ and $x - y = 3$}?

Here's How to Crack It

When combining equations, the goal is to eliminate one variable from the calculations. If a variable is eliminated, then we can easily solve for the other variable. To start, line up the two equations vertically:

$$3x + y = 5$$

$$x - y = 3$$

Take a look at the two equations and ask yourself if you can eliminate a variable by either adding or subtracting them. In the example above, we can add the two equations to eliminate the variable y:

$$\begin{array}{r} 3x + y = 5 \\ +\ x - y = 3 \\ \hline 4x = 8 \end{array}$$

Now that we have only one variable left, solve for x:

$$4x = 8$$

$$x = 2$$

So we have found the value of x. To find y, substitute the value of $x = 2$ back into either equation.

Now let's take a look at how two equations can be combined by subtracting one equation from another:

Find the solutions to the system:

$$3x + 4y = 11$$

$$x + 4y = 9$$

Here's How to Crack It

If you look at these two equations, you can see that addition will not help you eliminate a variable (the solution is $4x + 8y = 20$). The substitution method is one possible way to solve this system, but another way would be to subtract one equation from another. If you subtract the second equation from the first, you can eliminate y. Note that when you subtract an equation, the sign for every term changes. Another way to think about this is to multiply the entire equation by -1, and then add the two equations. So start with $-(x + 4y = 9)$, which is the same as $-x - 4y = -9$. Now add the equations:

$$\begin{array}{r} 3x + 4y = 11 \\ -x - 4y = -9 \\ \hline 2x = 2 \\ x = 1 \end{array}$$

With the value of $x = 1$, we can find the value of y:

$$x + 4y = 9$$

$$(1) + 4y = 9$$

$$4y = 8$$

$$y = 2$$

The solution set is (1, 2).

Finally, consider the following set of equations:

$$3x + 2y = 14$$

$$2x + 5y = 24$$

How would you solve this system of equations? Which one of the methods that we've discussed would help us solve this question? As you can see from the set of equations above, combining the equations through addition or subtraction will not eliminate a variable. In situations like this, one possible solution is to multiply an equation by a coefficient; we do this so that combining the two equations will allow us to eliminate a variable. There are almost an unlimited number of ways to multiply these equations, so choose numbers that will be easy for you to manipulate:

$$3x + 2y = 14$$

$$2x + 5y = 24$$

Let's multiply these equations by the following amounts:

$$-2(3x + 2y = 14) = -6x - 4y = -28$$

$$3(2x + 5y = 24) = 6x + 15y = 72$$

Now the equations are in a form such that combining them will allow us to eliminate a variable. After adding the two equations, we get:

$$0x + 11y = 44$$

$$11y = 44$$

$$y = 4$$

If $y = 4$, then:

$$3x + 2(4) = 14$$

$$3x + 8 = 14$$

$$3x = 6$$

$$x = 2$$

You could also have substituted the value for x into either of the equations that resulted from our multiplication coefficient—it would not have made any difference. The solution to the system of equations is (2, 4).

SIMPLIFYING RATIONAL EXPRESSIONS

A **rational number** is any number that can be expressed exactly by a ratio of two numbers, but don't worry about what this means right now. A **rational expression** is defined as a quotient of two different polynomials, and will always indicate division. Rational expressions have the same properties as rational numbers, so the rules for rational numbers apply to rational expressions. For example, in the rational expression $\dfrac{8}{y}$ there are a number of different possible values for y, but y cannot be 0. If it were, the value $\dfrac{8}{y}$ would not be a rational expression.

You will need to know how to simplify rational expressions in order to solve some problems on the GSE in Algebra. With these expressions, you can use the rules of factoring that we discussed above. Let's start with the following example:

$$\text{Simplify } \frac{y^2+5y+4}{3y+12}$$

Here's How to Crack It

A rational expression is in simplest form when the top part and the bottom part of the fraction have no common factors. Are there common factors in the problem above? At first glance, they may be difficult to see, but factoring the top and bottom parts of the fraction will help us determine if we can simplify it.

$$\frac{(y+4)(y+1)}{3(y+4)}$$

Now we can simplify the expression. The term $(y + 4)$ is common to both parts of the fraction, so let's cancel this term out and see what we get:

$$\frac{(y+1)}{3}$$

Factoring is crucial to simplifying rational expressions, but in addition to simplifying these expressions, you may be asked to add, subtract, multiply, or divide them. In any case, use factoring so to cancel or combine like terms.

Dividing Polynomials by Other Polynomials

What if you were asked to find the quotient in the expression:

$$\frac{x^2+5x+6}{3}$$

This would not be too challenging. Simplifying, you would divide each term on top by 3, which would give you the result:

$$\frac{x^2}{3} + \frac{5x}{3} + \frac{6}{3}$$

$$\frac{x^2}{3} + \frac{5x}{3} + 2$$

Not too bad. But how would you find the solution to this expression?

$$\frac{x^2 + 5x + 6}{x + 2}$$

When you have a rational expression that does not have a monomial as part of the denominator, you can use long division in order to simplify the expression. Set up the division like this:

$$x + 2 \overline{)x^2 + 5x + 6}$$

Your first step is to look at the values on the left of each polynomial. x^2 divided by x is x. Don't worry about any other part of the calculation yet. Right now, we have this:

$$x + 2 \overline{)x^2 + 5x + 6} \quad ^x$$

After we've completed this step, we need to multiply our partial quotient by the divisor. When we multiply x by $(x + 2)$, we get:

$$x^2 + 2x$$

Next, subtract this value from what we have in the dividend:

$$0x^2 + 3x$$

and bring down the next column of information

$$3x + 6$$

Again, look at the values on the far left of both the remainder and the divisor.

What is $\frac{3x}{x}$? It is 3. So place that value on top of the division sign:

$$
\begin{array}{r}
x + 3 \\
x + 2 \overline{)x^2 + 5x + 6} \\
\underline{x^2 + 2x} \\
3x + 6
\end{array}
$$

and multiply 3 now by $(x + 2)$:

$$3x + 6$$

and subtract. There is no remainder, and you have found that the quotient of

$\dfrac{x^2 + 5x + 6}{x + 2}$ is $(x + 3)$.

This method of long division is helpful if you have difficulty factoring. Further, it is helpful when polynomials are missing terms. Take the following example:

The result of $\dfrac{(y^3 + 1)}{(y + 1)} =$

A. y^2

B. $y^2 + 1$

C. $y^2 - y$

D. $y^2 - y + 1$

Here's How to Crack It

The expression above is difficult to factor, so let's try long division:

$$y + 1 \overline{) \, y^3 + 0y^2 + 0y + 1}$$

Notice that we've added two additional terms into the dividend. These are included to make the long division easier to do. Without them, you could get confused about where the numbers belong in your calculations. The complete solution is shown below:

$$
\begin{array}{r}
y^2 - y \qquad\; + 1 \\
y + 1 \overline{) \, y^3 + 0y^2 + 0y + 1} \\
\underline{y^3 + y^2} \\
-y^2 + 0y \\
\underline{-y^2 - y} \\
y + 1 \\
\underline{y + 1} \\
0
\end{array}
$$

By inserting the missing terms into the long division problem, our columns worked perfectly. The correct answer is D.

SIMULTANEOUS EQUATIONS IN WORD PROBLEMS

You will often need to use a system of equations when dealing with word problems on the GSE. While there are some specific strategies for word problems, you should also be familiar with how to set up simultaneous equations. We have already discussed how to solve a system of equations; now the challenge is to set up the equations properly. Consider the following example:

> Ben's music collection consists of both compact discs and cassettes. He has a total of 321 items in his music collection, and owns twice as many compact discs than cassettes. How many compact discs does Ben own?

Here's How to Crack It

One way to solve this problem would be to set up a series of equations. First let's define the variables:

$$\text{Let } \partial = \text{compact discs}$$

$$\text{Let } c = \text{cassettes}$$

The first statement tells us that the sum of compact discs and cassettes is 321:

$$c + \partial = 321$$

The second statement tells us that Ben owns twice as many compact discs as cassettes:

$$\partial = 2c$$

Thus, the two equations together are:

$$c + \partial = 321$$

$$\partial = 2c$$

Now substitute, and then solve for the variables.

$$c + 2c = 321$$

$$3c = 321$$

$$c = 107$$

Now, solve for ∂:

$$\partial = 2(107)$$

$$\partial = 214$$

COIN PROBLEMS

On the Algebra GSE, you might see some questions that deal with coins. Most of these questions can be solved with a system of equations. Below is one such example:

> Steve has a total of 21 coins, containing only dimes and nickels. If the total value of the coins is $1.70, then how many of each kind of coin does Steve have?

Here's How to Crack It

Again, to solve this problem, we need to write a series of equations. Defining the variables is fairly obvious:

$$\partial = \text{dimes} \qquad n = \text{nickels}$$

Our two equations are

$$\partial + n = 21$$

$$10\partial + 5n = 170$$

Let's talk about the second equation briefly. The total value of the dimes and nickels is $1.70, so we know that the combined value of dimes and nickels is $1.70. But the equation $\partial + n = \$1.70$ is incomplete. We need to associate these variables with values in order to make them equal. Think of everything in relation to 1 cent. In this case, a nickel has a value of $5n$ (5 times the number of nickels we have). Similarly, the value of dimes is 10∂. Finally, the value of $1.70 is 170 cents. Therefore, the second equation is written so that all variables and numbers are in the same units (cents).

Now let's solve the system of equations:

$$\partial + n = 21$$

$$10\partial + 5n = 170$$

$$10\partial + 5(21 - \partial) = 170$$

$$10\partial + 105 - 5\partial = 170$$

$$5\partial = 65$$

$$\partial = 13$$

If $\partial = 13$, then

$$13 + n = 21$$

$$n = 8$$

Make sure that you associate variables with their proper value in coin questions.

DIGIT PROBLEMS

Digit problems are similar to coin problems in that they require you to use a system of equations, and that you multiply variables by certain coefficients. Think of any two-digit number, such as 36. If you wanted to break this up into two different parts, you could use the units digit, 6, and the tens digit, 3. The two numbers 30 and 6, are placed together in order to create the number 36. Now, consider this with variables:

How is the term xy represented in an equation?

The value y is in the units place, while the value x is in the tens place. In order to express this two-digit number properly, it should be written as $10x + y$. Here's an example:

> The sum of the digits in a two-digit number is 12. If the digits were reversed, the new total would be 18 less than the original number. Find the original number.

Here's How to Crack It

With a two digit number, the sum can be represented by $x + y = 12$. For the second statement, we need to use the following equation:

$$10y + x = 10x + y - 18$$

The value $10x + y$ is that of our original number. When the digits are reversed, the new value is $10y + x$.

With these two equations, we can solve the system:

$$x + y = 12$$

$$10y + x = 10x + y - 18$$

$$x = 12 - y$$

$$10y + (12 - y) = 10(12 - y) + y - 18$$

$$10y + 12 - y = 120 - 10y + y - 18$$

$$9y + 12 = -9y + 102$$

$$18y = 90$$

$$y = 5$$

If $y = 5$, then:

$$x + y = 12$$

$$x + 5 = 12$$

$$x = 7$$

The original number is 75.

SUMMARY

Here's what you need to know regarding polynomials, factoring, and systems of equations:

1. Use columns to add and subtract polynomials. Remember that you can only combine like terms.

2. Be familiar with terms like coefficient, constant, and degree of term.

3. To multiply two polynomials, use the distributive property. Make sure each term in the one polynomial is multiplied by every term in the other polynomial.

4. Factoring does not change the value of an expression. Factoring rewrites a term into another form.

5. Use the FOIL method to expand a polynomial. Consider the reverse of the FOIL method when factoring a polynomial expression.

6. Remember the following three equations to help you quickly factor:

$$x^2 - y^2 = (x + y)(x - y)$$

$$x^2 + 2xy + y^2 = (x + y)^2$$

$$x^2 - 2xy + y^2 = (x - y)^2$$

7. Factoring can be a useful tool when solving equations. When factoring, you can set multiple terms equal to zero in order to find the possible solutions for an equation.

8. Remember how to set up a system of equations.

9. You can solve a system of equations through the following methods:

   a) substitution

   b) combining by addition or subtraction

   c) combining after multiplication

10. Recognize that simultaneous equations are often required to solve word problems but don't forget that you can also Backsolve.

11. Use long division to solve rational expressions when factoring may not be helpful. When there are missing terms, insert them with a coefficient of 0 into the dividend.

12. In coin and digit problems, give variables their proper units so that you create accurate equations.

GRAPHING

OVERVIEW

In this chapter, we'll discuss how to make visual representations of many of the algebraic expressions items we have seen in previous chapters. We will learn how to graph points, lines, equations, and inequalities. We will discuss the concept of slope, and then review specific rules for calculating the slope of different equations. We will also graph systems of equations to get an idea of their solution sets. Throughout this chapter and the next, we will review many concepts that are closely related to the study of geometry. The beauty (or challenge, depending how you look at it) of algebra is that it can be used in most branches of mathematics. To begin our study of graphing, we'll reintroduce something you learned about in elementary school—the number line.

CROSSING NUMBER LINES

On a number line, each point is a representation of a specific number. For example, on the number line below, the plot of the point (the dot) represents the number 3:

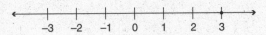

In order to plot many different points in space, we need to use more than one number line; we will want to use a graph. A graph is really nothing more than two intersecting number lines. A graph, also known as a **Cartesian system**, is shown below:

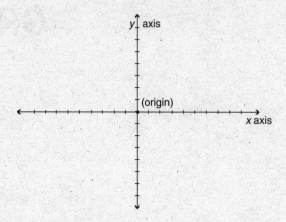

As you can see, this graph was formed by two intersecting number lines; one horizontal and one vertical. The horizontal line is known as the **x-axis**, and the vertical line is known as the **y-axis**. The two axes intersect at a point known as the **origin**. Every point on this graph has a corresponding pair of numbers, called coordinates, that tell you where a point is located on this plane. Look at the point labeled as (3, 4). The first number, 3, is the **x-coordinate**. It is a distance of 3 spaces to the right of the origin. A positive value means that you move to the right; a negative value means that you move to the left. The second number, 4, is the **y-coordinate**. It is a distance of 4 spaces above the origin. A positive value means that you move up from the origin; a negative value means that you move down from the origin.

To plot points on a graph, always start at the origin, moving the appropriate number of spaces across the x-axis (by looking at the x-coordinate), and the appropriate number of spaces up or down the y-axis (by looking at the value of the y-coordinate).

QUADRANTS

The coordinate plane is divided into four different regions that are created by the intersection of the two number lines. These regions are known as **quadrants**. Each quadrant is labeled with a specific number, moving counterclockwise from the upper-right hand side. The quadrants are labeled in the graph below:

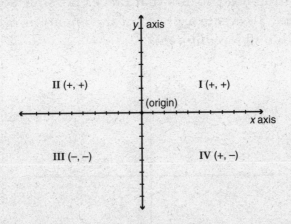

GRAPHING EQUATIONS

Think of the equation $2x + 4 = 12$. It will have only one solution: $x = 4$. We could plot the solution to this equation on a number line.

Now, look at the equation $2x + 4y = 12$. As we have already seen, a single equation with many variables will have many possible solutions. We can find solutions to this equation in many ways—by trying numbers in our heads, by starting at the number 0 and moving upward, etc. It is usually easiest to find solutions to equations like the ones above by simply choosing a number for one variable, and then using substitution to find the other value. For example:

$$2x + 4y = 12$$

If $x = 2$,	then $y =$	$2(2) + 4y = 12$:	$4y = 8$	$y = 2$
If $x = 3$,	then $y =$	$2(3) + 4y = 12$:	$4y = 6$	$y = 1.5$
If $x = 0$,	then $y =$	$2(0) + 4y = 12$:	$4y = 12$	$y = 3$
If $x = 6$,	then $y =$	$2(6) + 4y = 12$:	$4y = 0$	$y = 0$

Using the solutions above, we can state that some possible solutions to the equation $2x + 4y = 12$ are:

$$(2, 2)$$

$$(3, 1.5)$$

$$(0, 3)$$

$$(6, 0)$$

Graphing an equation is a process that places possible solutions for an equation together on a grid. To create a graph of the equation, we can plot the points onto a grid. The result will look like this:

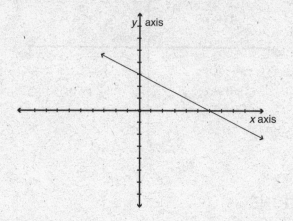

Now that you have plotted all the points, connect them, drawing a line through all the points, and going beyond the points you have plotted. You have just defined a line—a line is a figure used to connect points. Further, a line is continuous—it never ends. For example, did you know that the point (6000, –3000) is an ordered pair of the equation above? Try it. You will find that it fits. If we had lots of paper (and a lot more time!), we could plot this point on our graph. Lines are continuous, and include an infinite number of points.

If you are asked to graph an equation, it is usually helpful to plot a minimum of three points. Some people use a chart to keep track of their x and y coordinates, which isn't a bad idea. If you cannot get a straight line from those three points, check your math. Also, one easy way to find possible solutions for your equation is to locate the intercepts. Intercepts are points at which the equation crosses an axis. For example, if you set the value of $x = 0$, you will find the **y-intercept** (the value at which the graph crosses the y-axis). If you set the value of $y = 0$, you will find the **x-intercept** (the value at which the graph crosses the x-axis).

Linear Equations

Now that we have created a line from an equation, you may wonder if we can do this with every type of equation we're given. The answer is no. We dealt with a specific type of equation called a **linear equation**. So linear equations are equations whose graphs are straight lines. We can determine if an equation is linear by looking at its variables. In order for an equation to be linear:

1. x and y can only be to the first power (not squared, cubed, etc.)

2. the variables x and y can be added together, but not multiplied together

3. the variables x and y do not appear in the denominator

Here's an example:

> Which of the following equations is a linear equation:
>
> A. $y = (x-2)(x+2)$
>
> B. $y = \dfrac{2}{x}$
>
> C. $xy = 7$
>
> D. $-3x = 2 - y$

Here's How to Crack It

Answer choice A isn't linear because it contains the variable x to the second power. Answer choices B and C, when simplified, have x and y multiplied together. Only answer choice D meets the three conditions above.

Horizontal and Vertical Lines

We have mentioned that linear equations contain both an x value and a y value, so what would we do if we had the equation $x = 5$, or $y = 3$? Are these still linear equations? Can they be graphed?

The answer to both questions is yes. These equations are still linear, and they can be graphed. Think of the equation $x = 5$ as:

$$x + 0y = 5$$

When you attempt to find possible ordered pairs of solutions, you will see that you can choose anything for the value of y—it will not impact the equation. The following are all ordered pairs for the equation:

$$(5, 6)$$

$$(5, -30)$$

$$(5, 0)$$

$$(5, 1000)$$

$$(5, 23), \text{ etc.}$$

The graph of $x = 5$ is shown below. Notice that the graph is a vertical line.

A similar phenomenon occurs with the equation $y = 3$. It can be rewritten as:

$$0x + y = 3$$

The following are all ordered pairs for the equation:

(2, 3)

(5, 3)

(100, 3)

(0, 3)

(4, 3)

The graph of $y = 3$ is also shown in the graph below. Notice that the graph of this equation is a horizontal line. Finally, you should be able to tell that the point (5, 3) is common to both lines. This will become an important concept once we start solving for a system of equations of graphs.

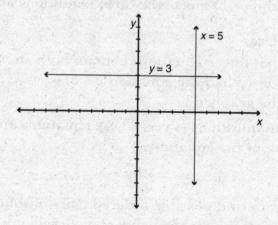

Slope

Now that we've seen how to graph linear equations, it's time to learn about an important measurement called slope. The slope of a line defines its steepness and direction. The **slope** (depicted by m) of a line is a ratio that compares the **rise** of a line to the **run** of a line. Given two points on a line, the change in the y coordinates is known as the rise. The change in the x coordinates is known as the run.

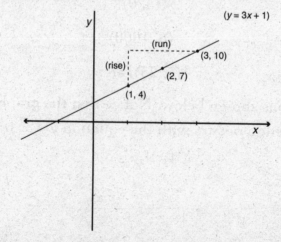

Take a look at two of the points on the line: (1, 4) and (3, 10). For the line above, the ratio of the rise to the run is 6 to 2. That is, $\frac{6}{2}$, or 3. The definition of slope is given below:

$$\text{Slope (m)} = \frac{\text{rise}}{\text{run}} = \frac{\text{difference of } y \text{ coordinates}}{\text{difference of } x \text{ coordinates}}$$

Now try a slope problem:

Find the slope of a line that contains the points (3, –4) and (5, –2)

Here's How to Crack It

While we could plot these points, draw a line through them, and count the rise and the run, it is usually easier to simply plug these values into our formula for slope. Using the definition of slope,

$$\text{Slope} = \frac{\text{rise}}{\text{run}} = \frac{((-2) - (-4))}{(5 - 3)} = \frac{2}{2} = 1$$

In order to find the slope in this problem, we took the difference of the y-coordinates and divided it by the difference of the x-coordinates. If you look at the math calculations above, you may wonder why we chose to subtract using the point (5, –2) first in our calculations. Actually, it would not matter which point we used first to find the difference. As long as you are consistent with your calculations, either ordered pair can be used first. If we solved the problem again by reversing the ordered pairs, we would get:

$$\text{Slope} = \frac{\text{rise}}{\text{run}} = \frac{((-4) - (-2))}{(3 - 5)} = \frac{-2}{-2} = 1$$

This realization gives us another way to define slope. It is called the **Difference of Two Points.** The definition is:

For any two points on a line, the points can be labeled (x_1, y_1) and (x_2, y_2). The slope of this line is found by the formula:

$$m = \frac{(y_2 - y_1)}{(x_2 - x_1)}$$

where m represents slope.

We have found the slope of one linear equation. Now let's go back to the lines we drew on page 100—the vertical line $x = 5$, and the horizontal line $y = 3$. How do we find their slopes?

Find the slope of the line $y = 3$

Here's How to Crack It

Start the process by choosing any two points on the line. For example, (1, 3) and (5, 3). Using the difference of two points formula, we have:

$$m = \frac{3 - 3}{5 - 1}$$

$$= \frac{0}{4}$$

$$= 0$$

(remember that 0 divided by any number equals 0)

There is no rise in this line. Therefore, we can say that: *Horizontal lines have a slope of 0.*

Now let's evaluate the vertical line $x = 5$:

Find the slope of the line $x = 5$

Here's How to Crack It

Start by choosing any two points on the line. For example, (5, 2) and (5, 7). Using the difference of two points formula, we have:

$$m = \frac{7 - 2}{5 - 5}$$

$$= \frac{5}{0}$$

$$= \text{undefined}$$

Division by 0 is not defined, and we can come to this conclusion: *Vertical lines do not have a slope.*

How is slope tested on the GSE? Often, you will need to use the difference of two points to find the values of a third point on a line. Here is an example:

A line contains points $(1, -1)$, $(3, 3)$ and $(x, -2)$. What is the value of x?

A. $-\dfrac{1}{2}$

B. $\dfrac{1}{2}$

C. 2

D. 4

Here's How to Crack It

The first step is to find the slope of the line. This can be found by taking the difference of the first two points:

$$slope = \frac{3 - (-1)}{3 - 1}$$
$$= \frac{4}{2}$$
$$= 2$$

Now that we know the slope is 2, we can set up an equation to find the value of x. You use the point that contains the variable, and one more point. (Again, you can choose either point.)

$$2 = \frac{-5}{(x - 3)}$$
$$2(x - 3) = -5$$
$$2x - 6 = -5$$
$$2x = 1$$
$$x = \frac{1}{2}$$

Answer choice B is correct.

The Slope-Intercept of a Line

There is a way to write a linear equation so that we immediately can tell the slope of the line. This form is called the slope-intercept equation. It is written as:

$$y = mx + b$$

In the equation above, m represents the slope, and b is the y-intercept. Remember that the y-intercept is the point at which the line hits the y-axis (the value of y when x is 0). Take a look at the equation below:

$$y = 2x + 5$$

From this equation, we know that the slope of this line is 2, and the y-intercept is 5.

This information gives us a way to immediately graph the linear equation, without having to find a series of ordered pairs. In order to graph this line, proceed this way:

1. Plot the point at the y-intercept. In our example above, this is (0, 5).

2. Use the slope to find the point at the value of $x = 1$. Use the rise/run calculation and the value for slope given in the slope-intercept equation.

3. Connect these points and graph the line of the linear equation.

The slope-intercept equation can be used to solve many algebra questions that you may encounter on the GSE. A common question asks you to create an equation for a line given some specific information. An example follows:

What is the equation of a line that has a slope of 3 and contains the point (7, 4)?

A. $y = 7x + 4$

B. $y = 4x - 7$

C. $y = 3x + 3$

D. $y = 3x - 17$

Here's How to Crack It
We can use the information that we're given in the equation and substitute it into the slope-intercept equation:

$$y = mx + b$$

$$4 = 3(7) + b$$

$$4 = 21 + b$$

$$-17 = b$$

Now that we have found the y-intercept of the equation, we can see that answer choice D gives us the correct answer.

Alternately, we could have used another equation, known as the point-slope equation:

$$y - y_1 = m(x - x_1)$$

Given one point and the slope, the point-slope equation allows us to determine the line of the equation. Using the numbers from above:

$$y - 4 = 3(x - 7)$$

$$y - 4 = 3x - 21$$

$$y = 3x - 17$$

So, given a point and the slope of a line, you can use either of these formulas to find the equation of the line.

Comparing Lines

So far we've focused on how to find the slope of a line and create equations from this information. But often, we want to have a way to compare the slope of one line to that of another. First let's distinguish between lines that have a positive slope, a negative slope, or zero slope. A line of each type is shown in the charts below:

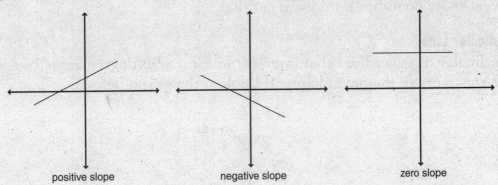

positive slope   negative slope   zero slope

A line that slopes up, to the right is said to have positive slope. That is, the number that expresses the rise over the run will be positive. A line that slants down (to the right) has a negative slope; the number that represents the rise over the run will be negative. Finally, a horizontal line has zero slope.

 ## Add This to Your Bag of Tricks!

One way to immediately eliminate answer choices in slope equations is to take a look at the direction of the line. For example, if a graphed line has a positive slope, you can quickly eliminate any answer choice that has a negative slope or negative number in its *m* position. This is just one way that you can save time on the GSE without performing a ton of calculations.

Parallel Lines

Parallel lines are lines that never intersect. These lines have the same slope and different y-intercepts. Take a look at the figure below:

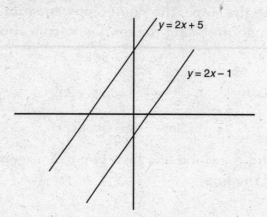

The lines in the figure above are parallel; they do not intersect, and each one has a slope of 2. In order to determine if two lines are parallel, first make sure that each line is in the $y = mx + b$ form. Next, compare their slopes to make sure they are equal, and their y-intercepts to make sure that they are different. If two lines meet these conditions, they are parallel.

Perpendicular Lines

Perpendicular lines are lines that intersect to form a 90-degree angle (we will discuss this more in the next chapter). Look at the graph below:

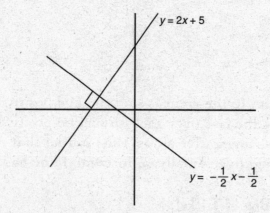

Two lines are perpendicular if they have reciprocal slopes. Remember that a reciprocal number is the opposite, or flipped version of a number. Two reciprocals multiplied together equal −1.

Here is a question, the likes of which you might see on the Algebra GSE:

Which of the following equations is perpendicular to the line $4y = 3x + 12$?

A. $y = 12x - 3$

B. $y = \dfrac{4}{3}x + 2$

C. $y = \dfrac{3}{4}x - 6$

D. $y = -\dfrac{4}{3}x - 2$

Here's How to Crack It

Remember that perpendicular lines have reciprocal slopes, so our first step is to find the slope of the given equation. To do this, we need to put it in $y = mx + b$ form:

$$4y = 3x + 12$$

$$y = \frac{3}{4}x + 3$$

We know that the slope is $\dfrac{3}{4}$. Therefore, we need to find an answer choice that has a slope of $-\dfrac{4}{3}$. Answer choice D is correct.

GRAPHING INEQUALITIES

So far, we have only graphed linear equations, but it is also possible to graph inequalities. Remember when we learned how to solve for an inequality? They were treated just like equations, but with a few extra rules. The same is true for graphing inequalities. Let's start with this inequality:

$$2x + 3y > 9$$

When we first dealt with linear equations, we were able to find many possible solutions to equations by listing ordered pairs. We can do the same with this inequality:

$$(10, 3)$$

$$(2, 4)$$

$$(-2, 8)$$

As you can see, there are an infinite number of solutions to the inequality above. With so many different points possible, it seems difficult to come up with a way to distinguish the solutions from the non-solutions. We can graph the solution set to this inequality by following the steps below:

1. Turn the inequality into an equality.

    So, in the example above, we work with the equation $2x + 3y = 9$

2. Plot points and draw a line for the equality

    Choose points like $(3, 1)$ $(0, 3)$ and $(\frac{3}{2}, 2)$. This will allow us to construct a graph of the line above.

3. Determine whether the line is a dotted line or a solid line. If the inequality uses the symbols > or <, then the line is dotted (the points on the line are *not* solutions to the inequality). If the inequality uses the symbols ≥ or ≤, then the line is solid (the points on the line are solutions to the inequality).

    In our example, the line is a dotted line; this expression contains the symbol >.

4. Shade the appropriate region to show where the solution set exists. The solution set must lie on one side of the equality line that you have drawn. One way to determine the location of the shaded region is by testing any point on the graph. If the point keeps the inequality true, then that side of the equality line should be shaded. We recommend trying the origin as your "test point"—it is easy to calculate, and by having a consistent test point you'll save time.

    In the example above, the origin $(0, 0)$ is not a possible solution to the inequality. Therefore, the shaded region is above the line, not below it.

A complete graph to our example is shown below:

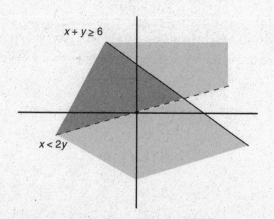

To summarize, we graphed the solution set to the inequality by first creating a line. The line was dotted because the equation contained the symbol >. Next, we shaded the region *above* the line because the point we tried below the line, (0, 0), did not keep the inequality true.

 Put This in Your Bag of Tricks!

Most Algebra GSE questions on this topic will give you the graph of an inequality and then ask you to choose the appropriate equation in the answer choices. In order to quickly eliminate answer choices, use the following properties of the graph:

- Is the line solid or dotted? Eliminate all answer choices do not represent the line that is drawn in this way.

- Does the line have an easily recognizable point in its solution set? Pick a point that is in the shaded area of the graph, and plug it into the answer choices. If it does not work, eliminate that equation.

These questions are best solved using Process of Elimination. Work intelligently on them to save as much time as possible!

GRAPHING A SYSTEM OF INEQUALITIES

Now that we have shown how to graph an inequality, and shade the solution set, we can now use a graph to represent the solution set of a system of inequalities. When you graph more than one inequality, you determine the shaded region by shading the overlap of the two regions. An example is shown below:

Graph the solution set of the system:

$$x < 2y$$

$$x + y \leq 6$$

Here's How to Crack It
The first step is to turn each inequality into an equality and find ordered pairs that fit each equation:

$x = 2y$	$x + y = 6$
(0, 0)	(2, 4)
(4, 2)	(4, 2)
(2, 1)	(0, 6)

Now graph each equation. As you graph the equations, remember that the line $x < 2y$ will be dotted, and the line $x + y \leq 6$ will be solid.

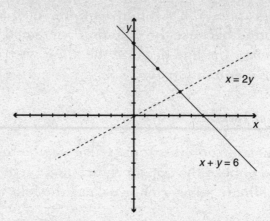

Now that you have the two lines, you need to determine the shaded region of each line separately. The shaded region of $x + y \leq 6$ will be below the line; the shaded region of $x < 2y$ will be above the line. Shade each region, as shown in the figure above.

Now look for the parts of the shaded regions that overlap. The correct answer is one in which the shaded area is above $x < 2y$ and to the left of $x + y \leq 6$.

If you want to make sure you have the right answer, use a test point from this region and plug it into both equations.

SUMMARY

1. A graph is created by the intersection of two number lines. The Cartesian grid system plots points of ordered pairs, in the form (x, y)

2. Linear equations have specific properties. Their variables are not raised to a power greater than one; their variables are not multiplied together, and the variables do not appear in the denominator.

3. Slope (m) is one measurement of a line that defines its steepness. It describes how quickly the rise over the run changes in a line. $m = \dfrac{\text{rise}}{\text{run}}$

4. The difference of two points states that slope can be determined from two points on a line: Given (x_1, y_1) and (x_2, y_2), the slope of the line is $\dfrac{(y_2 - y_1)}{(x_2 - x_1)}$.

5. Parallel lines are lines that do not intersect. They have the same slope, and different y-intercept values.

6. Perpendicular lines do intersect; they form 90-degree angles at the point of their intersection. Perpendicular lines have reciprocal slopes — their slopes, multiplied together, equal –1.

7. The slope-intercept equation is helpful in creating equations with information about the slope of a line, and one point on the line:

$$y = mx + b$$

8. Inequalities, like linear equations, can be graphed.

9. A graph of an inequality is either a solid line or a dotted line, depending on the sign used in the inequality < or > signs give dotted lines, while ≤ or ≥ give solid lines.

10. The "point test" can be used to help determine the solution region of an inequality.

11. When graphing a system of inequalities, the shared shaded region is the solution set to the system, and should be shaded.

7

GEOMETRY

OVERVIEW

Geometry? Aren't we preparing for the GSE in *Algebra*? Well, yes, but while the exam will test you primarily on algebra concepts, it will often test those concepts in the context of geometry problems. Therefore, you need to review the fundamentals of geometry so that you can solve these algebra questions.

We already tackled some minor geometry topics in the last chapter; we discussed the slope of lines at some length. We will continue to expand on slope this chapter, in addition to the other basic geometric concepts.

You may be somewhat nervous if you have not yet taken a Geometry course at your high school. No problem. While you will need to study this material in detail, it is not very complex. The most difficult parts about geometry—proofs, theorems, and complicated formulas—will *not* be tested on the GSE. But you will need to learn a few basic rules to learn to handle the approximately five to seven questions you will see on the test. The key to geometry questions is Process of Elimination! It is easy to recognize bad answer choices in these questions, so even if you aren't sure how to get the correct answer, start by eliminating as many answer choices as possible.

POINTS AND LINES

In the previous chapter, we discussed these two vital geometry terms. **Points** represent a location in space, and a **line** is a figure drawn to connect points together.

When a point extends into a line, this is called a **ray**. Rays, like lines, go on forever, but they go on forever only in one direction. A ray is shown below:

DEGREES

A degree is a unit of measurement in an angle. An angle is formed when two lines, or two rays, come together. A line has a degree measurement of 180 degrees. This piece of information is crucial to understanding how all geometric figures come together.

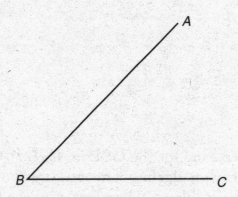

This angle can be depicted by $\angle ABC$. The point B is called the vertex of the angle. The vertex is the point at which the two lines meet to form an angle. When you name an angle, you always use the point of the vertex as the middle letter. Sometimes, you will also see an angle labeled with just the vertex letter, such as $\angle B$.

There are a few names for angles.

- If an angle is less than 90 degrees, it is called an **acute angle**.

- If an angle is equal to 90 degrees, it is called a **right angle**. These angles are the type of angles formed when two perpendicular lines intersect (we discussed this in the last chapter). Right angles will be frequently seen in our discussion of triangles.

- If an angle is greater than 90 degrees, it is called an **obtuse angle**.

There are many more detailed rules and terms to describe the properties of angles, in the study of geometry, but on the Algebra GSE, you will not need to have a vast knowledge of angles. You will only need to know how angles work in a series of shapes.

TRIANGLES

Every triangle contains 180 degrees. The word triangle means *three angles*, and every triangle contains three interior angles. These angles will always sum to exactly 180 degrees. Don't worry about why or how. Just know that the three angles will always sum to 180 degrees.

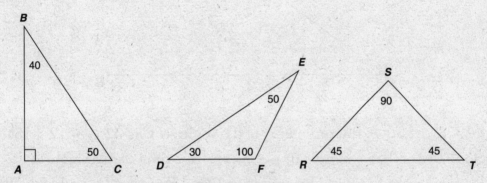

A problem on the GSE might look like this:

The values of the angles in a triangle are $(2x + 8)$, $(3x - 1)$, and $(3x + 13)$. What is the value of the smallest angle in the triangle?

A. 20

B. 48

C. 59

D. 71

Here's How to Crack It

To find the smallest angle, we first need to find the value of x. To do this, we need to sum the angles together. From the rule of triangles above, we know that the sum of the angles will equal 180:

$$180 = (2x + 8) + (3x - 1) + (3x + 13)$$

$$180 = (2x + 3x + 3x) + (8 - 1 + 13)$$

$$180 = 8x + 20$$

$$160 = 8x$$

$$20 = x$$

Since $20 = x$, we can substitute to find that the angles equal 48, 59, and 73. Answer choice B is correct.

The perimeter of a triangle is the sum of the lengths of its sides. Finding the perimeter of a triangle is pretty simple—just add the lengths of the three sides.

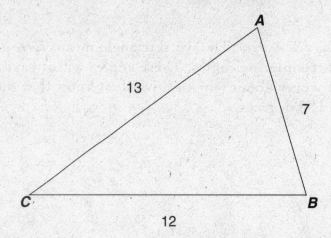

In the picture above, the perimeter of Triangle *ABC* is 32 (7 + 12 + 13).

Let's look at another example of perimeter, this time using algebra:

The lengths of the sides of a triangle are $(2x + 3)$, $(4x + 7)$, and $(5x - 2)$. What is the perimeter of the triangle?

Here's How to Crack It

To find the perimeter, simply add all the sides together. In the problem above, we have:

$$\text{Perimeter} = (2x + 3) + (4x + 7) + (5x - 2)$$

$$= (2x + 4x + 5x) + (3 + 7 - 2)$$

$$= 11x + 8$$

The area of a triangle is defined as $\dfrac{1}{2} \cdot height \cdot base.$

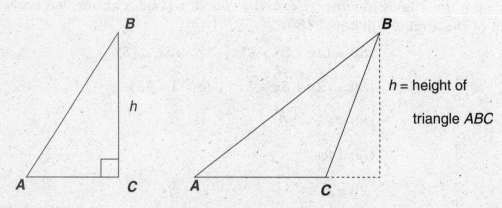

h = height of

triangle *ABC*

The base (*b*) of a triangle is defined as one side of the triangle. In general, the base is the bottom side of the triangle. In the pictures above, *AC* is the base. The height, or *h*, is defined as the length from the base to the highest point in the triangle. In some cases, the height can be represented by one of the sides of the triangle, as in the first triangle (line *BC* covers the length from the top of the triangle to the base *AC*), but the height may not always be represented by one of the sides of the triangle. In the second example, the height reaches from point *B* to the base. That line, however, is not one of the sides of the triangle.

The most common mistake in calculating the area of a triangle is to forget to multiply by $\frac{1}{2}$. Always write down the formula before you attempt to solve a triangle area question!

There are several "special" triangles—including isosceles, equilateral, and right triangles. An **isosceles** triangle is a triangle in which two angles are equal, which means that their corresponding sides are also equal. An **equilateral** triangle goes one further—all of the angles and sides are equal (meaning that the angles are all 60 degrees). Finally, a **right** triangle contains one angle that is 90 degrees (a right angle). Here is a picture of a right triangle:

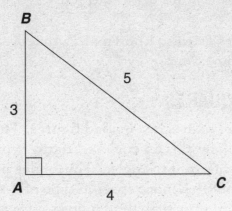

Right triangle *ABC*

Right Triangles

Right triangles have some special properties. By knowing a few rules, you can easily find the values of all the angles in a right triangle, as well as the lengths of its sides. You can find the lengths of the sides by knowing a special rule, called the **Pythagorean theorem**. Here is what the Pythagorean theorem says:

In a right triangle with sides *a*, *b*, and hypotenuse *c*, $a^2 + b^2 = c^2$.

First let's define the word **hypotenuse**. The hypotenuse is the longest side of a right triangle (the other sides are commonly called **legs**). It can be found opposite the 90-degree angle (since the 90-degree angle is the largest angle, it is always opposite the longest side—another rule for triangles). If we look back at our picture, you can see that the calculations prove the Pythagorean theorem:

$$3 \cdot 3 + 4 \cdot 4 = 5 \cdot 5$$

$$9 + 16 = 25$$

$$25 = 25$$

Therefore, if you are given any two sides of a right triangle, you will be able to find the third side. But wait just a second! On the GSE, the authors love to use the same types of right triangles again and again. If you learn about these triangles, you won't have to worry about lots of calculations. Below are some of the most common right triangles:

$$3\text{-}4\text{-}5$$

$$6\text{-}8\text{-}10$$
(and any other multiple of a 3-4-5 triangle)

$$5\text{-}12\text{-}13$$

$$7\text{-}24\text{-}25$$

These common values are also known as Pythagorean Triplets. If you memorize them, you'll save some time.

RECTANGLES AND SQUARES

There are many different names for 4-sided figures. The most generic term is **quadrilateral**. A quadrilateral is an enclosed figure with four sides; quadrilaterals can be cut into two different triangles. The angles in a quadrilateral add up to 360 degrees (2 · 180 = 360). A more specific type of 4-sided figure is a parallelogram. A **parallelogram** is a quadrilateral whose sides are two sets of parallel lines. Further, the opposite angles in a parallelogram are equal. Rectangles and squares are specific types of parallelogram in which all of the angles were 90 degrees. Because these types of figures are the most common 4-sided figures to show up on the Algebra GSE, we will review their properties in detail.

Rectangles and squares are special types of parallelograms in which all the angles are right angles. In addition to containing only right angles, rectangles and squares both have equal opposite sides, and all opposite sides are parallel to one another. A square has four equal sides.

Here is an example of a question you might see on the GSE:

> If $(3x + 9)$ is the measure of one of the angles
> in a rectangle, then what is the value of x?
>
> A. 27
>
> B. 54
>
> C. 108
>
> D. 216

Here's How to Crack It

We know that all of the angles in a rectangle must equal 90 degrees, so we can set the term equal to 90 and solve for x:

$$3x + 9 = 90$$

$$3x = 81$$

$$x = 27$$

Answer choice A is the correct answer.

The perimeter of a rectangle or a square is the sum of the lengths of its sides.

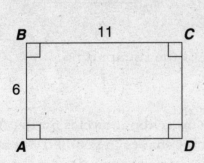
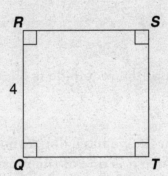

In the figures above, the perimeter of the rectangle is 34 and the perimeter of the square is 16.

An algebra question on the GSE might look like this:

> The length of a rectangle is $(3x - 7)$. The
> width of a rectangle is $(2x + 4)$. What is the
> perimeter of the rectangle?
>
> A. $5x - 3$
>
> B. $10x - 6$
>
> C. $6x^2 - 28$
>
> D. $6x^2 - 2x - 28$

Here's How to Crack It

The perimeter of a rectangle is twice the sum of its length and width. Start by adding the length and width together:

$$(3x - 7) + (2x + 4) =$$

$$5x - 3$$

To get the perimeter, multiply this by 2:

$$2 \cdot (5x - 3) = 10x - 6$$

Answer choice B is correct answer.

To find the area of a rectangle, multiply the length and width; to find the area of a square, square the length of one side.

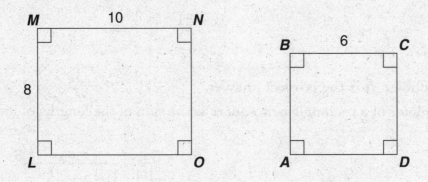

The area of the rectangle is 80; the area of the square is 36.

CIRCLES

In our research, we have not seen any questions about circles on the Algebra GSE, but since it is one of the most important shapes in geometry, it might just show up in the future: the curriculum guides state that circles can be tested on this test. We've put some of the facts you should know about circles below—you probably won't need them, but here they are, just in case.

Circles contain 360 degrees. Every circle, regardless of size, adds up to 360 degrees. A line from the center of the circle to any point on the outside of the circle is called a **radius**. All radii within a circle are of equal length. The common abbreviation of a radius is *r*. A **diameter** is defined as a line that reaches from one point on the circle to another point on the circle, passing through the radius. The diameter, or *d*, is twice the length of the radius. All diameters within a circle are of equal length.

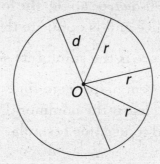

The key to any circle question is to know the value of the radius. You will need this value to find the circle's circumference and its area. The **circumference** of a circle is $2\pi r$, or πd, where r is the radius of the circle and d is the diameter. The area of a circle is πr^2, where r is the radius of the circle. Try this problem:

O is the center of the circle below. Find the circle's circumference and its area:

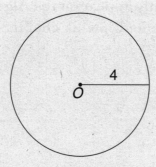

First let's find the circumference. The radius of the circle is 4. Knowing this, we can find the circumference:

$$2\pi r = 2\pi(4) = 8\pi$$

Next, we can find the area of the circle:

$$\pi r^2 = \pi(4)^2 = 16\pi$$

SUMMARY

1. Certain algebra questions on the exam involve geometry shapes and figures, so in this chapter we're making sure you are familiar with the basics of geometry.

2. A line has 180 degrees. Angles are formed by placing two lines or two rays together.

3. Triangles have three angles that always sum to 180 degrees.

4. A right angle has one 90-degree angle; the longest side in a right angle is named the hypotenuse and is opposite the right angle.

5. The perimeter of a figure is the sum of its sides.

6. The Pythagorean theorem helps us to find the lengths of the sides in a right triangle. If you learn the common Pythagorean Triplets, you will probably not need to use this formula.

7. The area of a triangle is $\frac{1}{2} b \cdot h$.

8. Rectangles and squares are four-sided figures with special properties. All of the angles in rectangles and squares are 90 degrees.

9. The perimeter of a rectangle is $2(l + w)$. The area of a rectangle is $l \cdot w$.

10. The perimeter of a square is $4s$. The area of a square is s^2.

11. Circles do not frequently appear on the Algebra GSE, but you should learn the basics presented in this chapter in case you encounter a circle problem.

8

SPECIAL TOPICS

OVERVIEW

Believe it or not, we have already covered about 85 percent of all the material that will appear on the Algebra GSE. In this chapter, we are going to cover some of the more difficult, more abstract concepts that may appear on the exam. Unlike previous chapters, these concepts will not build on each other, so feel free to jump around this chapter as needed. If you have trouble with any of these concepts, keep in mind that no single area within this chapter will appear with great frequency. We're just including this content review to ensure that no question will take you by surprise when you tackle the Algebra GSE.

A quick piece of advice: This chapter ranks as the least important for you to know in this book. If you have any questions about Chapters 1–7, we recommend that you study those again before tackling this chapter.

SCIENTIFIC NOTATION

Scientific notation is another shorthand way to represent very large or very small numbers. How far is it from San Francisco to Los Angeles, in inches? If you calculated an estimated value, you would get tired from writing zero after zero after zero, because the number would be so large. When there are so many numbers to work with, it becomes much easier to make an error. To provide a more efficient way of labeling numbers, we use a form called scientific notation.

Scientific notation uses a number as a product of the power of 10. For example, let's start with the following numbers:

$$62{,}500 \qquad .056$$

In scientific notation, the first number would be written as 6.25×10^4, and the second number would be written as 5.6×10^{-2}.

How do you translate a number in standard notation to scientific notation, and vice versa? In order to translate numbers, go through the following steps:

1. Move the decimal place from its current location to the right of a units digit. You want your number to have a units digit, followed by the decimal sign.

2. Count the number of places you traveled to get to that point.

3. This number of places becomes your power of 10. *If you moved the decimal to the left, the power is positive; if you moved the decimal to the right, the power is negative.*

4. Combine the number and the power of 10.

Let's do another example using the four steps we outlined above:

How do you write the number 12,600 in scientific notation?

Here's How to Crack It

Using the steps we mentioned above;

1. Move the decimal, so the number becomes 1.2600

2. Count the number of places we moved it — we moved it four spaces

3. Because we moved it to the left, the power of 10 will be 10^4

4. The solution is 1.26×10^4 (you can drop the 0s after the 6 in the number).

Now that we have determined how to translate to scientific notation for one expression, we can do an example where we combine expressions. Consider the following example:

Simplify the following expression:
$(3.2 \times 10^{-5})(2.0 \times 10^8)$

Here's How to Crack It

When asked to combine numbers written in scientific notation together, treat the numbers and the powers separately.

$$(3.2 \times 2)(10^{-5} \times 10^8)$$

$$(6.4) \times (10^3)$$

$$6.4 \times 10^3$$

Note: Many calculators allow you to enter numbers in scientific notation. Most have something similar to an **EXP** button. This button will allow you to solve and combine numbers in scientific notation. To solve the problem above using a calculator, do the following:

$$3.2 \ \textbf{EXP} \ -5 \ \times 2.0 \ \textbf{EXP} \ 8 =$$

You should see a read out of something like 6.43 or 6.4×10^3.

WORK, RATE, AND MIXTURE PROBLEMS

The GSE may test you on three specific types of word problems. We will cover each type of word problem in detail, and show you what you need to do in order to set up a rational equation (or system of equations) for these problems. We've combined the three different types of questions here because they all involve similar concepts and equations.

Work Problems

Let's assume that you're working on a homework assignment, and that it takes you a total of four hours to complete that assignment. If you work at a steady rate, then you complete one-fourth of the job per hour. Defining rates in which a person can complete certain jobs is helpful in many of the work problems you'll see. By defining a rate, you can compare work performances for various individuals. Now consider the following problem:

> Ben can build a desk in six hours. Alex can build a desk in eight hours. If Ben and Alex work together, how long would it take them to build a desk?
>
> A. $3\dfrac{3}{7}$ hours
>
> B. 4 hours
>
> C. $6\dfrac{2}{7}$ hours
>
> D. 14 hours

Here's How to Crack It

We need to define a rate for both Ben and Alex in order to use their performance together:

Ben performs $\dfrac{1}{6}$ of the job per hour.

Alex performs $\dfrac{1}{8}$ of the job per hour.

Because we have defined both of their work performances in fractional terms, we can now combine them to figure out how long it takes for them to complete the desk.

$$\frac{1}{6} + \frac{1}{8} =$$

$$\frac{4}{24} + \frac{3}{24} = \frac{7}{24}$$

Together, they complete $\frac{7}{24}$ of the job in one hour. To find the total time it takes them, take the reciprocal of this number. It takes them $\frac{24}{7}$ hours in order to complete this job. Choice A is the correct answer.

How did we know that the amount of time it took to complete the job was the reciprocal of their rate? Well, consider the following equation:

$$\frac{\text{Amount of Job}}{\text{Hour}} \times \text{Hour} = \text{Job}$$

Substituting into the equation above, we have:

$$\frac{7}{24} \times H = 1$$

$$H = \frac{24}{7}$$

(The Job = 1 because we are completing one job; that is, building one desk.) Let's do one more example of a work problem:

> Gretchen can complete the payroll in 3 hours. Working with Laurie, Gretchen and
>
> Laurie can complete payroll together in $\frac{15}{11}$ hours. How long would it take Laurie, working alone, to complete the payroll?
>
> A.   3 hours
>
> B.   2.5 hours
>
> C.   1 hour
>
> D.   24 minutes

Here's How to Crack It

This question is slightly more complicated than the previous one. We know that Gretchen's rate is $\frac{1}{3}$. We also know that Gretchen's rate plus Laurie's rate is $\frac{15}{11}$. How did we know this? Remember that the time to complete the job and the rate are reciprocals. Therefore, we can set up the following equation:

$$G + L = \frac{11}{15}$$

$$\frac{1}{3} + L = \frac{11}{15}$$

$$\frac{5}{15} + L = \frac{11}{15}$$

$$L = \frac{6}{15}, \text{ or } \frac{2}{5}$$

Laurie's rate is $\frac{2}{5}$. Notice that this is not the correct answer (watch out for answer choice D—this is Laurie's rate.) So if she can do $\frac{2}{5}$ of the job per hour, then it will take her the reciprocal, or $\frac{5}{2}$ hours, to complete the job. Answer choice B is correct.

Rate Problems

The work problem above was an example of a special type of rate problem. To figure out how long it would take to complete a job, we multiplied the amount of $\frac{job}{hour}$ times hours worked. This provides the foundation for most rate problems.

You are probably most familiar with the following equation:

$$R \times T = D$$

or

rate × *time* = *distance*

Most algebra examples using rate and time on the GSE talk about traveling in a car. Some rate questions are simply proportions. For example:

A car travels at 30 miles per hour. How far will the car have traveled after 4 hours?

Here's How to Crack It

This question is simply a proportion. We can set up an equation to show the following:

$$\frac{30 \text{ miles}}{1 \text{ hour}} = \frac{x \text{ miles}}{4 \text{ hours}}$$

You could cross multiply to find that $30(4) = 1(x)$

$$120 = x$$

There are other rate questions that will require to you to do more than simply construct a proportion. Here's an example of one:

One car travels 20 miles per hour faster than another car. The faster car travels a total distance of 140 miles, while the slower car travels a total distance of 80 miles. Assuming both cars started at the same time, how long were the cars traveling?

Here's How to Crack It

One of the easiest ways to solve this type of rate question is to make a chart for the information that you're given from the problem. A sample chart is shown below:

	Rate	Time	Distance
Slower Car	r	t	80 miles
Faster Car	$r + 20$	t	140 miles

We have assigned variables to represent the information that we do not know. We know that the rate of the faster car is 20 miles per hour faster than the slower car, so we can label the two rates r and $r + 20$. The time for each car is the same, so we can use the same variable for time.

Now how do we solve this equation? Let's start by using our rate formula:

$$r \times t = d$$

For the slower car, we have:

$$rt = 80$$

For the faster car, we have:

$$(r + 20)(t) = 140$$

Because the time is equal in both equations, we can isolate t in each expression, and then set the two equations equal to each other, as follows:

$$T = \frac{80}{r}$$

$$T = \frac{140}{r + 20}$$

Therefore,

$$\frac{80}{r} = \frac{140}{r + 20}$$

Cross multiply to solve for r:

$$80(r + 20) = 140r$$

$$80r + 1600 = 140r$$

$$1600 = 60r$$

$$\frac{1600}{60} = r$$

$$\frac{80}{3} = r$$

The rate of the slower car is $\frac{80}{3}$ miles per hour. We can put in the value of r into either equation to solve for the value of t:

$$t = \frac{80}{r}$$

$$t = \frac{80}{\frac{80}{3}}$$

$$t = 80\left(\frac{3}{80}\right) = 3$$

The amount of time the cars have been traveling is 3 hours.

Mixtures

The key to solving a mixture problem is to clearly label all pieces of information. We recommend using a table similar to the one we showed you above for Rate questions. Here is a sample mixture question:

> At the Juice Factory, a solution containing 30% orange juice is to be mixed with a solution containing 50% orange juice to make 200L of a solution containing 42% orange juice. How much of the 50% solution needs to be used?

Here's How to Crack It

In the problem above, we're given values for the percentages of orange juice in the solutions. We are also given complete information about the final solution. We need to determine the amount of solution needed in order to get the desired final solution. Use a table like the one shown below:

	Amount of Solution	Percent of Orange Juice	Amount of Orange Juice
1st Solution	x	50%	$.5x$
2nd Solution	$200 - x$	30%	$60 - .3x$
3rd Solution	200	42%	$(.42)(200)$

We can create an equality from the given information. The amount of orange juice in the first solution plus the amount of orange juice in the second solution will give us the solution:

$$.5x + (60 - .3x) = .42 \times 200$$

$$.5x + 60 - .3x = 84$$

$$.2x = 24$$

$$x = 120$$

Therefore, the solution requires 120L of the 50% solution and 80L of the 30% solution.

Working with Square Roots

Throughout this review, we have dealt with numbers that have been raised to the second power. For example, x^2 is the squared value of x. Sometimes, however, we will need to find the square root of a number.

A square root can be represented with two different terms. The most common symbolic representation of a square root sign is $\sqrt{\ }$. Another way to represent a square root is to raise the power to a fractional amount.

$$\sqrt{x} \text{ is the same as } x^{\frac{1}{2}}$$

On the GSE, you will only be asked to find the positive square root of a number. For example, $\sqrt{25}$ is equal to 5.

You are probably familiar with square roots. You have already used them for factoring polynomials. Here, we'll focus on using square roots in many of the same exercises we have done in previous chapters—simplifying expressions, multiplying expressions, dividing expressions, and performing an operation called rationalizing.

Simplifying Square Roots

When an expression is written under a radical, or square root sign, it is called a radical expression. These radical expressions, like any other expression, can often be simplified. First we'll tell you a few rules about square roots: *The square root of any number is either 0 or positive.* Therefore, there are a few values that do not give a real number solution. For example, $\sqrt{-16}$ is not a real number. On the GSE, you will only be tested about real numbers. Sometimes you will asked to determine which values for a variable can exist so that the expression produces a real number solution. For example:

Which of the following inequalities gives all real number solutions to the expression $\sqrt{x+2}$?

A. $x = 7$

B. $x > 2$

C. $x > -2$

D. $x \geq -2$

Here's How to Crack It

The value underneath a square root sign must produce a result that is either positive or zero. Therefore, for any term underneath a square root sign, we can define the possible values by setting the expression as greater than or equal to 0. So we have:

$$x + 2 \geq 0$$

$$x \geq -2$$

and answer choice D is correct. Any number that's −2 or greater, will produce a real number solution for the expression.

Simplifying a radical expression is similar to simplifying any polynomial expression. Consider the following example:

Simplify: $\sqrt{x^2 + 8x + 16}$

Here's How to Crack It

First, completely ignore the square root sign. Focus only on the expression that you see underneath the sign:

$$x^2 + 8x + 16$$

Can this term be factored? Yes it can. This polynomial can be simplified to

$$(x + 4)(x + 4) \text{ or } (x + 4)^2$$

So the expression now looks like this:

$$\sqrt{(x + 4)^2}$$

The correct answer is $(x + 4)$.

This example brings up a rule that you should remember: *For any real number a*, $\sqrt{a^2} = a$.

This means that the square root of a number squared is equal to the number. The same is true for polynomial expressions, as we saw in our example above.

Multiplying Radical Expressions

When you multiply two radical expressions, follow these steps:

1. Multiply everything together first, ignoring the square root sign.

2. Once you have combined the values into one radical expression, try to simplify.

Don't try to factor out values for each individual radical expression first. This will take up unnecessary time. Try this example:

What is the value of $\sqrt{(12x^3y^2)(3x^2y^6)}$

Here's How to Crack It

Using our rules above, the first thing we do is combine the terms:

$$\left(\sqrt{36}\right)\left(\sqrt{x^5}\right)\left(\sqrt{y^8}\right)$$

Now we can simplify by taking the square root of each term:

$$(6)\left(x^{\frac{5}{2}}\right)(y^4)$$

Dividing Radical Expressions

To divide two radical expressions, use the same two-step process that we used to multiply radical expressions:

1. Divide everything together first, ignoring the square root sign.

2. Once you have combined the values into one radical expression, try to simplify.

First we'll demonstrate how division works with radical expressions by taking a look at a fraction:

$$\text{What is } \sqrt{\frac{9}{25}} \text{ ?}$$

When you try to simplify a radical expression that includes division, take the square root of both the top part and the bottom part of the fraction, as follows:

$$\frac{\sqrt{9}}{\sqrt{25}} = \frac{3}{5}$$

Now let's try this with two different radical expressions:

$$\text{What is } \sqrt{\frac{8x^4}{32x^2}}$$

Here's How to Crack It

The first step is to divide the terms without worrying about the square root sign:

$$\frac{8x^4}{32x^2} = \frac{x^2}{4}$$

Next, take the square root of $\frac{x^2}{4}$:

$$\sqrt{\frac{x^2}{4}} = \frac{\sqrt{x^2}}{\sqrt{4}} = \frac{x}{2}$$

$\frac{x}{2}$ is the answer.

Rationalizing an Expression

Sometimes when you're working with radical expressions, you will find that the denominator contains a radical. Unfortunately, any expression that contains a radical in the denominator is not in simplified form. This is important because you will not see an expression of this type in the answer choices. Therefore, in addition to making sure you have reduced the expression as much as possible, you will need to make sure that there is not a square root sign in the denominator.

Sometimes, you will need to use an equality to remove a radical from the denominator. This process is called rationalizing. Let's take a look at an example of rationalizing a number:

$$\text{Simplify } \frac{\sqrt{2}}{\sqrt{3}}$$

Here's How to Crack It

This expression is not simplified, because there is a radical sign in the denominator. How can we eliminate the $\sqrt{3}$ from the bottom part of the equation? One way is to multiply both the numerator and denominator by $\sqrt{3}$, as follows:

$$\frac{\sqrt{2}}{\sqrt{3}} = \left(\frac{\sqrt{2}}{\sqrt{3}}\right)\left(\frac{\sqrt{3}}{\sqrt{3}}\right)$$

$$= \frac{\left(\sqrt{2}\right)\left(\sqrt{3}\right)}{\left(\sqrt{3}\right)\left(\sqrt{3}\right)}$$

$$= \frac{\sqrt{6}}{3}$$

In order to rationalize the expression, multiply the expression by the radical in the denominator.

Adding and Subtracting

Finally, let's spend a minute reviewing how to combine radical expressions through addition and subtraction. In general, it is easiest to think of radical expressions like variables—you can only combine like terms. Consider the following examples:

$$4x + 5y = 9x$$

$$4\sqrt{3} = 5\sqrt{3} = 9\sqrt{3}$$

$$4x + 5y \text{ can not be simplified}$$

$$4\sqrt{3} + 5\sqrt{2} \text{ can not be simplified}$$

The same rule holds true with subtraction. To finish our review of radical expressions, let's do a problem that combines many of the rules we've discussed above:

Simplify the following expression:

$$\sqrt{(x^3 - x^2)} + \sqrt{4x - 4}$$

Here's How to Crack It

The expression can be simplified as follows:

$$\sqrt{(x^3 - x^2)} + \sqrt{4x - 4}$$
$$= \sqrt{x^2(x - 1)} + \sqrt{4(x - 1)}$$
$$= x\sqrt{x - 1} + 2\sqrt{x - 1}$$
$$= x + 2\sqrt{x - 1}$$

Equations with Radical Expressions

To solve equations with radicals, we first need to convert them to equations *without* radicals. To do this, we need to square both sides of an equation. Consider the following equation to be solved:

$$3 + \sqrt{x - 1} = 5$$

Here's How to Crack It

First, as always, isolate the variable from the remainder of the equation:

$$\sqrt{x - 1} = 2$$

Now, we need to square both sides of the equation:

$$x - 1 = 4$$
$$x = 5$$

QUADRATIC EQUATIONS

In Chapter 6, we discussed functions, and the graphs of functions. In algebra, you will see many problems that discuss a specific type of function, called a quadratic function. In general, a quadratic function is in the form:

$$y = ax^2 + bx + c$$

where a, b, and c are real numbers. This specific type of function usually takes the form of a **parabola** when graphed.

Standard Form

Quadratic equations are said to be in standard form when the value of y in the equation above is set equal to 0. To solve for quadratic equations, your first step should always be to ensure that they are in standard form. Try putting the following equation in standard form:

$$4x^2 = -8x - 5$$

In standard form, this equation is written as

$$4x^2 + 8x + 5 = 0$$

We can solve quadratic equations once they are written in standard form. Take a look at the question below:

What is the solution for x if $16x^2 - 12x = 0$?

Here's How to Crack It

First, this equation is in standard form, so we can start solving. We want to factor the polynomial expression as much as possible. After factoring, we get:

$$4x(4x - 3) = 0$$

Now we can set each value equal to 0. This property is called the principle of zero products. If either $4x = 0$ or $4x - 3 = 0$, the entire equation will equal 0. Set each value equal to 0:

$$4x = 0 \qquad\qquad 4x - 3 = 0$$

$$x = 0 \qquad\qquad x = \frac{3}{4}$$

The solutions to the quadratic equation above are 0 and $\frac{3}{4}$.

Next, let's do another example in which the c value is not equal to zero:

What is the solution for y if
$3y^2 + 4y - 3 = y^2 + 3y + 12$?

Here's How to Crack It

Our first step is to get the equation in standard form:

$$3y^2 + 4y - 3 = y^2 + 3y + 12$$

$$2y^2 + y - 15 = 0$$

Next, see if you can factor the polynomial expression. You can:

$$(2y - 5)(y + 3) = 0$$

Set each term equal to 0:

$$2y - 5 = 0 \qquad\qquad y + 3 = 0$$

$$y = \frac{5}{2} \qquad y = -3$$

The solutions to this quadratic equation are -3 and $\frac{5}{2}$.

When Factoring Isn't Enough

Consider the following equation:

$$x^2 - 4x - 7 = 0$$

How do we solve for the value of x in the equation? If you try to factor, you'll find that you will not be able to come up with a way to simplify this further. Two numbers need to have a product of -7 and a sum of -4, but unfortunately, there are no integers that will satisfy the condition.

Remember that we can manipulate equations, as long as we do the same thing to both sides. In order to factor this equation further, we will need to alter it. One technique that's commonly used to solve these types of quadratic equations is called **Completing the Square.** Start by taking another look at the equation:

$$x^2 - 4x - 7 = 0$$

Before we complete the square, an equation must be in standard form. Further, the coefficient of the x^2 term (also known as the leading term) must be 1. If it isn't, divide the equation to make the first coefficient 1. Because those two conditions are met in our equation, we can start the process of completing the square. First, move the coefficient to the right side of the equation:

$$x^2 - 4x = 7$$

Next, look at the second term in the equation: $-4x$.

Divide this term by 2 to get $-2x$.

Take the coefficient and square it: $(-2)(-2) = 4$.

Add this value to both sides of the equation:

$$x^2 - 4x + 4 = 11$$

Next, factor the perfect square we have just created:

$$(x - 2)(x - 2) = 11$$

Simplify:

$$(x - 2)^2 = 11$$

Take the square root of both sides:

$$x - 2 = \pm\sqrt{11}$$

Solve for the value of x:

$$x = 2 + \sqrt{11}, \text{ and } 2 - \sqrt{11}$$

Let's do one more example to make sure you understand the rules for completing the square:

$$\text{What is } x \text{ if } x^2 + 8x - 2 = 0?$$

Here's How to Crack It

In order to clarify the process for completing the square, we have written our explanation in steps:

Step 1: Is the equation in standard form? Yes.

Step 2: Can it be factored using integers? No. We can't find two integers that have a product of –2 and a sum of 8. Therefore, we need to complete the square.

Step 3: We need to move the constant to the right hand side of the equation:

$$x^2 + 8x = 2$$

Step 4: Focus on the middle term: $8x$; half of the coefficient is 4

Step 5: Square the coefficient: 16

Step 6: Add this to both sides of the equation:

$$x^2 + 8x + 16 = 18$$

Step 7: Factor:

$$(x + 4)(x + 4) = 18$$

$$(x + 4)^2 = 18$$

Step 8: Take the square root of both sides:

$$x + 4 = \pm \sqrt{18}$$

$$x = \sqrt{18} - 4 \quad \text{and} \quad -\sqrt{18} - 4$$

The Quadratic Formula

As you have seen from the steps above, there is a specific pattern to the way in which we can solve a quadratic equation using completing the square. Well, mathematicians have come up with an equation that will always give us a tool to find the solutions of a quadratic equation:

For a quadratic equation written in the form $ax^2 + bx + c = 0$, the solutions to x are found with the formula:

$$x = \frac{-b \pm \sqrt{b^2 - 4ac}}{2a}$$

This is the quadratic equation. You should memorize it. It's long, but once you know it, you will have a failsafe way to find the solutions to any quadratic equation. Try this example:

Solve the equation $3x^2 + 2x - 7 = 0$ using the quadratic equation.

Here's How to Crack It

Identify the coefficients in the equation above:

$$a = 3 \qquad b = 2 \qquad c = -7$$

Next, substitute into the quadratic formula:

$$x = \frac{-2 \pm \sqrt{(2)^2 - 4(3)(-7)}}{2(3)}$$

$$x = \frac{-2 \pm \sqrt{4 + 84}}{6}$$

$$x = \frac{2\left(-1 \pm \sqrt{22}\right)}{6}$$

$$x = \frac{-1 \pm \sqrt{22}}{3}$$

Yes, that number is pretty ugly! You can expect to see values like this appear on the GSE after you use the quadratic equation. The challenge is to keep track of all the different values you need to plug into the quadratic formula.

 The Discriminant

So far, every quadratic equation that we've solved has had two real number solutions, but some quadratic equations will have 0 or 1 real number solutions. In order to determine the number of solutions quickly, you do not need to use the entire quadratic formula. Instead, you can use part of it, called the **discriminant**. The discriminant is:

$$b^2 - 4ac$$

This is what using the discriminant tells us:

- If $b^2 - 4ac$ is positive, there are two real-number solutions.

- If $b^2 - 4ac$ is negative, there are no real-number solutions.

- If $b^2 - 4ac$ is zero, there is one real-number solution.

You should memorize this information so that you can quickly evaluate the number of solutions to a quadratic equation. *Add this to your Bag of Tricks!*

Let's say you have the same question from above, but with the following answer choices:

> The solution to the equation $3x^2 + 2x - 7 = 0$ is:
>
> A. $x = 3$
>
> B. $x = 0, 3, 5$
>
> C. $x = \dfrac{-1 \pm \sqrt{22}}{3}$
>
> D. There are no real-number solutions for the value of x.

To solve this question quickly, use the discriminant. The value of the discriminant, $b^2 - 4ac$, is:

$$2^2 - 4(3)(-7)$$

which is a positive number. That means there are two solutions. Only answer choice C contains two solutions. You've found the correct answer without using the quadratic formula!

PROBABILITY

Probability is a large and complicated branch of mathematics. If you choose to continue your math studies in college, you can take an entire year of classes simply devoted to probability and statistics. Obviously, the GSE won't test you on nearly that much, but you may see a few questions about probability.

Probability is a mathematical representation of the likelihood of an event. To represent the probability of an event, we need to know the possible number of outcomes. Since most probability questions deal with either dice or cards, we'll focus our examples on these two things. Let's say that you have a die, with faces painted 1, 2, 3, 4, 5, and 6. If you role the die, how many different outcomes could there be? There are six possible outcomes. Let's say that you wanted to know the odds, or the probability, of the number 3 appearing when you throw the die. Since the number 3 is just as likely to show up as 1, 2, 4, 5, or 6, the probability of rolling a 3 is $\frac{1}{6}$. This example helps us to define probability:

$$\text{probability} = \frac{\#\ \text{of desired outcomes}}{\text{total}\ \#\ \text{of outcomes}}$$

Probability always has a value between 0 and 1. A probability of 0 means that there is no chance for a certain outcome; for example, what is the probability that when you throw the die you get a 7? A probability of 1 means that there is absolute certainty for a certain outcome, for example, what is the probability that when you throw the die you get a number less than 10?

Before we do a few examples with probability, here is some information about common sources of probability questions:

- **Coins:** A coin has two different outcomes, heads and tails.

- **Dice:** A die contains six sides, numbered 1, 2, 3, 4, 5, and 6

- **Cards:** A deck of cards consists of 52 cards. Of these 52 cards, there are four different suits—hearts, diamonds, spades, and clubs. Hearts and diamonds are red; spades and clubs are black. Each suit has the following cards: 2, 3, 4, 5, 6, 7, 8, 9, 10, J, Q, K, A

Here's an example:

If a die is thrown, what is the probability that an even number will appear?

Here's How to Crack It
We know that there are six possible outcomes: 1, 2, 3, 4, 5, and 6

There are three possible even outcomes: 2, 4, and 6 are all even, so the probability is $\frac{3}{6}$, or $\frac{1}{2}$.

Combining Multiple Probability Events
Sometimes you will be asked questions about the probability of a *series* of events. There are some events that will not have an impact on the outcome of other events. These are called complementary events. One such example of complementary events is flipping a coin. Consider the following example:

Rachel was flipping a coin. On each of her first three tosses, heads appeared. What is the probability that she will get heads again on her next throw?

Here's How to Crack It

The probability of getting heads when flipping a coin is $\frac{1}{2}$. This probability is constant, regardless of previous outcomes; the result of the previous coin flips does nothing to change the outcome of the next coin toss. This is an example of complementary events.

Sometimes, you'll be asked to find the probability of two events occurring. If these events cannot happen at the same time, they are called mutually exclusive events. For example, if a die is tossed, the outcome of a 3 and the outcome of a 5 are mutually exclusive—they both cannot occur at the same time. We can find the chance that either a 3 or a 5 will appear by adding their individual probabilities:

$$\text{probability of a 3} = \frac{1}{6}$$

$$\text{probability of a 5} = \frac{1}{6}$$

So, the probability of either a 3 or a 5 appearing is equal to

$$\frac{1}{6} + \frac{1}{6} = \frac{1}{3}$$

Let's now say that I want to know the probability of rolling a 3 twice in a row. To find this probability, I need to break down the question into its individual events:

What is the probability of getting a 3 on the first throw? $\frac{1}{6}$

What is the probability of getting a 3 on the second throw? $\frac{1}{6}$

If I want to know the probability of rolling a 3 twice in a row, I need to multiply these two terms together:

$$\left(\frac{1}{6}\right)\left(\frac{1}{6}\right) = \frac{1}{36}$$

When combining the probabilities of different events, multiply the probabilities to find the odds that *both* events will occur.

Finally, look at this last type of question:

Lesly has a jar of marbles. There are 6 black marbles and 8 red marbles. If Lesly randomly picks 2 marbles out of the jar, what is the probability that Lesly will choose 2 red marbles?

Here's How to Crack It

To calculate the probability that she'll choose two red marbles, we need to first calculate the probability that she will get a red marble on her first draw, and then calculate the probability of getting a red marble on her second draw.

First draw: There are a total of 14 marbles, and 8 are red, so the probability is $\frac{8}{14}$, or $\frac{2}{7}$.

Second draw: Assuming that Lesly got a red marble on her first draw, how many marbles are left? 13. Remember, we have removed one of the marbles, so we are down to 13. How many red marbles are left? 7 (one red marble was removed in the first draw). So the probability of getting a red marble on the second draw is $\frac{7}{13}$.

Multiply the combined probability:

$$\left(\frac{2}{7}\right)\left(\frac{7}{13}\right) = \frac{2}{13}$$

and the correct answer is $\frac{2}{13}$.

ORGANIZATION OF DATA

If you have a bunch of numbers or calculations, it is often helpful to have a way to organize them. Below, we will discuss a few methods of organizing statistical data, and how to answer GSE questions about data.

Stem-and-Leaf Diagrams

Imagine that you had collected a series of data. The numbers that you have collected are listed below:

145, 162, 149, 151, 139, 172, 147, 151,
136, 165, 169, 140, 150, 139, 171, 155, 152

If you look at this data, you can see that the numbers are similar to each other in value. Many of the numbers are in the 140s, 150s, etc. When numbers are close to each other, one way to organize them is to construct a stem-and-leaf diagram. A stem-and-leaf diagram separates each number into two parts. A completed diagram is shown below:

Stem	Leaf
13	6, 9, 9
14	0, 5, 7, 9
15	0, 1, 1, 2, 5
16	2, 5, 9
17	1, 2

In the diagram above, the term **stem** refers to the first two digits in the number. The term **leaf** is the final digit in the number. This chart allows us to quickly locate the range of numbers given in the set of data. We can find the smallest number, 136, and the largest number, 172, quickly.

On the GSE, you may be presented a stem-and-leaf diagram and asked to identify certain properties of the numbers. You may be asked to find the smallest or largest number, or the number that shows up with the most frequency.

Scatter Plots

A scatter plot is a graph that shows the relationship between two variables. Scatter plots can be used to determine whether or not a relationship exists between two sets of variables.

Consider the charts below:

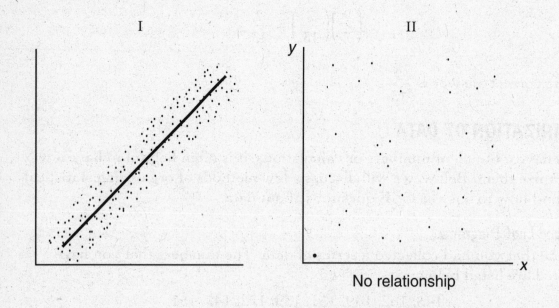

When evaluating scatter plots, you will be asked to determine if one of the following relationships exists:

Positive relationships: That is, as one variable increases, the other variable increases. Positive relationships will look like Chart I. As the value of x increases, the value of y increases. If you were to draw a line that best represented the points in the scatter plot, you would find that the line has positive slope. A sample line is drawn in the first chart to demonstrate this.

Negative relationships: A negative relationship means that as one variable increases, the other variable decreases. A line drawn through the points listed in the scatter plot would have a negative slope.

No relationship: When the scatter plot does not clearly show a pattern of points, the two variables are said to have no relationship. Chart II gives you one example where there is no clear relationship between the two variables.

SUMMARY

After completing this chapter, you should know the following:

1. Scientific notation can be used to simplify very large or very small numbers. Follow the four steps outlined earlier in this chapter to convert a number to scientific notation.

2. Work problems require that you determine a rate for each worker.

3. The work rate and time to complete a job are reciprocals of each other.

4. Rate questions commonly use the equation $r \times t = \partial$. Use a chart to fill in all of the information you are given before determining an equation.

5. Mixture questions are a special type of rate problem. Use a chart to determine an equation.

6. You should now be able to add, subtract, multiply, and divide with square roots.

7. A simplified expression will never have a radical in its denominator. Use a technique called "rationalizing" to remove a radical from the denominator.

8. Quadratic equations are in the form $ax^2 + bx + c = 0$.

9. The first step to solving quadratics is to put them in their standard form.

10. If you cannot factor a quadratic equation, you can use the method of "completing the square" to find the solution set.

11. Memorize the quadratic formula so that you can solve any quadratic equation quickly.

12. Use the discriminant to determine the number of real-number solutions in a quadratic equation.

13. Probability is always between 0 and 1. It is defined as

$$\frac{\text{\# of defined outcomes}}{\text{total \# of outcomes}}.$$

14. Stem-and-leaf plots are used to summarize similar data.

15. Scatter plots are used to determine whether a relationship exists between two variables.

Part III

THE PRINCETON REVIEW
ALGEBRA GSE
PRACTICE TEST I

SESSION ONE

Directions

Make sure you have two or three No. 2 pencils with erasers and a ruler or straightedge available to you during the exam. You also may have a calculator; it may be either a scientific or graphing calculator. You may not use minicomputers, pocket organizers, or calculators with QWERTY (typewriter) keyboards. You may not share your calculator with other students.

Do not spend too much time on a question that seems too difficult. Answer the easier questions first and then return to the harder ones if you have the time. Try to answer every question, even if you have to guess.

Notes:

(1) Figures that accompany problems are drawn as accurately as possible EXCEPT when it is stated that a figure is not drawn to scale. All figures lie in a plane unless otherwise indicated.

(2) All numbers used are real numbers. All algebraic expressions represent real numbers unless otherwise indicated.

1. Solve the following equation, and give the answer to the nearest tenth:

$$6x + 6 = 17 - 3(x - 3)$$

   A. 2

   B. 2.2

   C. 6.6

   D. 6.7

2. Evaluate $(3x)^3 + 4$ for $x = 2$:

   A. 22

   B. 28

   C. 216

   D. 220

3. Solve the following equation for x, and round to the nearest tenth:

$$\frac{1}{2}x - \frac{3}{5} = \frac{1}{10} + \frac{3}{5}$$

   A. 1.3

   B. 2.6

   C. 3.9

   D. 5.0

4. The value in dimes of $(2x - 2)$ dollars is:

   A. $200x - 200$

   B. $50x - 50$

   C. $20x - 20$

   D. $2x - 2$

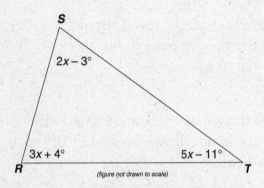

(figure not drawn to scale)

5. Triangle *RST* has angles with the indicated measures. What is the value of its largest angle?

   A. $19°$

   B. $61°$

   C. $84°$

   D. $180°$

6. At the chocolate factory, dark chocolate costs $3 per pound and white chocolate costs $5 per pound. If the factory were to make a mixture that costs $4.20 per pound, what percent of white chocolate would be used?

   A. 24%

   B. 40%

   C. 60%

   D. 76%

7. Which of the following equations represents a line passing through $(-3, 4)$ and $(-5, 2)$?

   A. $x - y = -7$

   B. $-3x + 4y = 25$

   C. $-2x + 4y = 18$

   D. $2y - 5x = 29$

8. Which of the following answer choices correctly factors $x^2 - 13x - 30$?

   A. $(x - 10)(x - 3)$

   B. $(x - 6)(x - 7)$

   C. $(x + 15)(x - 2)$

   D. $(x + 2)(x - 15)$

9. Kathleen and Elizabeth jog a total of 23 miles today. If Kathleen jogs 5 more miles than Elizabeth, how many miles did Elizabeth jog?

   A. 5

   B. 9

   C. 14

   D. 16

10. Chris and Peter were the only two candidates for president of the school pre-medical club. If 416 votes were cast, and Chris received 38 more votes than Peter, how many votes did Peter receive?

    A. 38

    B. 189

    C. 227

    D. 378

11. The solution of $|4x + 3| = 5$ is:

    A. $-\dfrac{1}{2}$

    B. $\dfrac{1}{2}$

    C. 2

    D. $\dfrac{1}{2}, -2$

12. If $\dfrac{2x-5}{3} = \dfrac{x+7}{2}$, then $x =$

    A. 5

    B. 7

    C. 17

    D. 31

13. What is the perimeter of a triangle with lengths $(3x - 4)$, $(2x + 9)$, and $(8 - 2x)$?

    A. $7x + 21$

    B. $7x + 13$

    C. $3x + 21$

    D. $3x + 13$

14. Which of the following lines is perpendicular to the line $3y = 9x + 3$?

    A. $6y + 2x = 6$

    B. $6y = 18x + 6$

    C. $3y = 3x + 9$

    D. $10y + 2x = 12$

15. The total area of a figure is $8b^2 - b + 8$. There are three regions to the figure: Region I has area of $4b^2 + 5b + 2$. Region II has area of $b^2 + b - 3$. What is the area of Region III?

    A. $3b^2 - 7b + 9$

    B. $3b^2 - 5b + 7$

    C. $3b^2 - 7b + 3$

    D. $\dfrac{8}{5}b^2 - \dfrac{1}{6}b + 8$

16. Tim roles a die and gets a three. What is the probability that the next throw will NOT be a three?

    A. 1

    B. $\dfrac{5}{6}$

    C. $\dfrac{1}{2}$

    D. $\dfrac{1}{3}$

17. A line passes through the following points: $(5, -2)$, $(-1, -6)$, and $(4, k)$. What is the value of k?

    A. -4

    B. $\dfrac{2}{3}$

    C. $\dfrac{3}{2}$

    D. $-\dfrac{8}{3}$

18. What is the value of y if $\sqrt{y+6} = 8$

    A. 2

    B. 10

    C. $\dfrac{8}{3}$

    D. 58

19. If (x, y) is the solution of the system of equations $\{x - 2y = 9, 2x + y = 8\}$, then the value of $x + y$ is:

A. 3

B. 5

C. 8

D. 16

20. The of solution(s) to $5x^2 - 8x = -3$ is(are):

A. $\left(\dfrac{3}{5}, 1\right)$

B. 1

C. $-\dfrac{5}{3}$

D. -3

21. If x is a real number such that $0 < x < 3$, and $y = \dfrac{x^2}{2}$, then which of the following gives the complete range of the equation?

A. $0 < y < \dfrac{9}{2}$

B. $-\dfrac{2}{3} < y < 1$

C. $y < \dfrac{9}{2}$

D. $y > 0$

22. If $b = 5$, then find the value of $\dfrac{b^2 + b}{2b}$.

A. 1.5

B. 3

C. 5

D. 5.5

23. Simplify the following expression:

$$(3a^4b^5c^6d^{-2})^3$$

A. $9a^7b^8c^9d$

B. $9a^{12}b^{15}c^{18}d^{-6}$

C. $27a^7b^8c^9d^6$

D. $27a^{12}b^{15}c^{18}d^{-6}$

24 and 25: For the questions below, use the following stem-and-leaf diagram:

Stem	Leaf
16	9
17	2, 8
18	3, 3, 3, 4, 6
19	0, 5, 6, 8, 9
20	1, 1, 3

24. The above stem-and-leaf diagram is a set of heights, in centimeters, of players on a high-school basketball team. What height shows up the most frequently?

A. 3

B. 18

C. 183

D. 201

25. If you were to pick a number at random from the stem-and-leaf diagram above, what is the probability that the number would end in a 3?

A. $\dfrac{3}{18}$

B. $\dfrac{3}{16}$

C. $\dfrac{1}{4}$

D. $\dfrac{2}{5}$

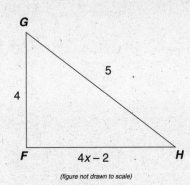

G

5

4

F   4x − 2   H

(figure not drawn to scale)

26. If the area of triangle *FGH* is 36, what is the value of *x*?

    A. 5

    B. 9

    C. 12

    D. 18

27. When the factored polynomial $(x + 3)(x + 4)$ is expanded, the result is $x^2 + 7x + r$. What is the value of *r*?

    A. 7

    B. 12

    C. 19

    D. 24

28. Which of the following lines is parallel to the line represented by $y = -3x + 4$ and passes through point $(-3, 11)$?

    A. $6x + 2y = -10$

    B. $2y = -6x + 4$

    C. $12x + 4y = 7$

    D. $y = -3x + 11$

29. Marty has two numbered cubes, each numbered 1–6. What is the probability that when the cubes are tossed, the total will be an 8?

    A. $\dfrac{1}{12}$

    B. $\dfrac{5}{12}$

    C. $\dfrac{5}{36}$

    D. $\dfrac{1}{6}$

30. The product of $\sqrt{2a}$ and $\sqrt{8a}$ is:

    A. $4a$

    B. $4a^2$

    C. $16a$

    D. $16a^2$

1

YOUR NAME: _____
(Print)
     Last   First   M.I.

SIGNATURE: _____ DATE: ____ / ____ / ____

HOME ADDRESS: _____
(Print)
         Number and Street

_____
   City   State   Zip Code

PHONE NO.: _____
(Print)

Completely darken bubbles with a No. 2 pencil. If you make a mistake, be sure to erase mark completely. Erase all stray marks.

Practice Test I

1. Ⓐ Ⓑ Ⓒ Ⓓ   16. Ⓐ Ⓑ Ⓒ Ⓓ
2. Ⓐ Ⓑ Ⓒ Ⓓ   17. Ⓐ Ⓑ Ⓒ Ⓓ
3. Ⓐ Ⓑ Ⓒ Ⓓ   18. Ⓐ Ⓑ Ⓒ Ⓓ
4. Ⓐ Ⓑ Ⓒ Ⓓ   19. Ⓐ Ⓑ Ⓒ Ⓓ
5. Ⓐ Ⓑ Ⓒ Ⓓ   20. Ⓐ Ⓑ Ⓒ Ⓓ
6. Ⓐ Ⓑ Ⓒ Ⓓ   21. Ⓐ Ⓑ Ⓒ Ⓓ
7. Ⓐ Ⓑ Ⓒ Ⓓ   22. Ⓐ Ⓑ Ⓒ Ⓓ
8. Ⓐ Ⓑ Ⓒ Ⓓ   23. Ⓐ Ⓑ Ⓒ Ⓓ
9. Ⓐ Ⓑ Ⓒ Ⓓ   24. Ⓐ Ⓑ Ⓒ Ⓓ
10. Ⓐ Ⓑ Ⓒ Ⓓ   25. Ⓐ Ⓑ Ⓒ Ⓓ
11. Ⓐ Ⓑ Ⓒ Ⓓ   26. Ⓐ Ⓑ Ⓒ Ⓓ
12. Ⓐ Ⓑ Ⓒ Ⓓ   27. Ⓐ Ⓑ Ⓒ Ⓓ
13. Ⓐ Ⓑ Ⓒ Ⓓ   28. Ⓐ Ⓑ Ⓒ Ⓓ
14. Ⓐ Ⓑ Ⓒ Ⓓ   29. Ⓐ Ⓑ Ⓒ Ⓓ
15. Ⓐ Ⓑ Ⓒ Ⓓ   30. Ⓐ Ⓑ Ⓒ Ⓓ

GRID-IN ANSWER SHEET

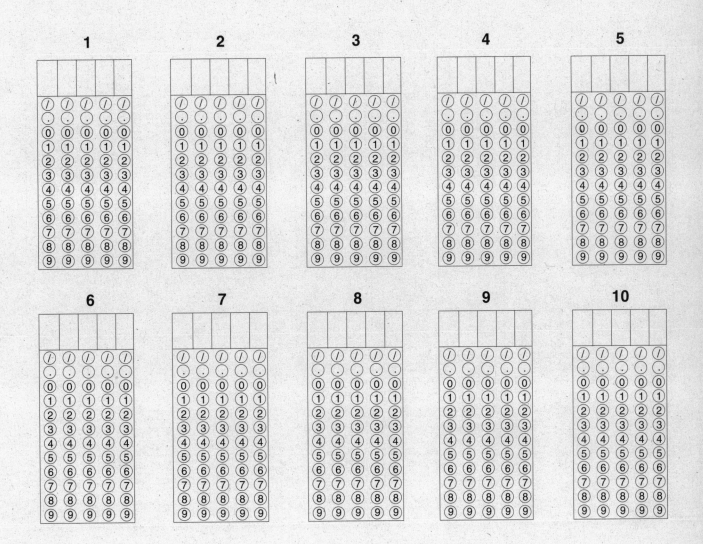

WRITTEN RESPONSE
ANSWER SHEET

ANSWERS AND EXPLANATIONS FOR SESSION ONE

Answer Key

1.	B	11.	D	21.	A
2.	D	12.	D	22.	B
3.	B	13.	D	23.	D
4.	C	14.	A	24.	C
5.	C	15.	A	25.	C
6.	C	16.	B	26.	A
7.	A	17.	D	27.	B
8.	D	18.	D	28.	B
9.	B	19.	A	29.	C
10.	B	20.	A	30.	A

Explanations

1. Solve the following equation, and give the answer to the nearest tenth:

$$6x + 6 = 17 - 3(x - 3)$$

A. 2

B. 2.2

C. 6.6

D. 6.7

1. The correct answer is B. Remember to use your calculator, especially if the problem indicates that you will need to round off (that is usually a sign that the numbers won't be easily calculated):

$$6x + 6 = 17 - 3x + 9$$

$$6x + 6 = 26 - 3x$$

$$9x = 20$$

$$x = \frac{20}{9} \text{, or } 2.22222$$

2. Evaluate $(3x)^3 + 4$ for $x = 2$:

A. 22

B. 28

C. 216

D. 220

2. The correct answer is D. Evaluate the expression using the order of operations:

$$(3 \times 2)^3 + 4$$

$$6^3 + 4$$

$$216 + 4$$

$$220$$

Remember, **P**arenthesis, **E**xponents, **M**ultiplication and **D**ivision, **A**ddition and **S**ubtraction (**PEMDAS**)

3. Solve the following equation for x, and round to the nearest tenth:

$$\frac{1}{2}x - \frac{3}{5} = \frac{1}{10} + \frac{3}{5}$$

A. 1.3

B. 2.6

C. 3.9

D. 5.0

3. Choice B is the correct answer. You can add fractions together using your calculator, you can also Backsolve to find the correct answer, or you could manipulate the equation in the following way:

$$\frac{1}{2}x - \frac{3}{5} = \frac{1}{10} + \frac{3}{5}$$

$$\frac{1}{2}x = \frac{1}{10} + \frac{3}{5} + \frac{3}{5}$$

$$\frac{1}{2}x = \frac{1}{10} + \frac{6}{10} + \frac{6}{10}$$

$$\frac{1}{2}x = \frac{13}{10}$$

$$2 \cdot \frac{1}{2}x = \frac{13}{10} \cdot 2$$

$$x = \frac{26}{10}$$

$$x = 2.6$$

4. The value in dimes of $(2x - 2)$ dollars is:

A. $200x - 200$

B. $50x - 50$

C. $20x - 20$

D. $2x - 2$

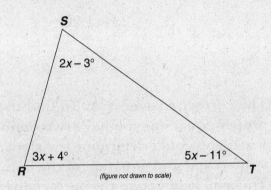

S

$2x - 3°$

$3x + 4°$ $5x - 11°$

R   (figure not drawn to scale)   T

5. Triangle *RST* has angles with the indicated measures. What is the value of its largest angle?

A. $19°$

B. $61°$

C. $84°$

D. $180°$

4. Choice C is the correct answer. This question asks us to take an algebraic expression and change the expression by using a different set of units. Here the expression is originally in dollars, which is 10 times the value of dimes (there are 10 dimes for one dollar). To change the expression, multiply the entire expression by 10:

$$10(2x - 2) = 20x - 20$$

5. Choice C is correct. The angles in a triangle add up to 180 degrees. First sum the angles to solve for x:

$$(2x - 3) + (3x + 4) + (5x - 11) = 180$$

$$10x - 10 = 180$$

$$10x = 190$$

$$x = 19$$

Next, substitute the value of 19 for each of the angles. You can probably tell that $2x - 3$ won't be the largest angle. After substitution, the angles are 35, 61, and 84. 84 is the largest angle.

6. At the chocolate factory, dark chocolate costs $3 per pound and white chocolate costs $5 per pound. If the factory were to make a mixture that costs $4.20 per pound, what percent of white chocolate would be used?

   A. 24%

   B. 40%

   C. 60%

   D. 76%

6. The correct answer is C. Before we got to an equation, remember to Ballpark. If the two chocolates were used in equal amounts, the cost would be $4 per pound. However, because the cost is more than $4, we know that more of the more expensive white chocolate was used. Eliminate answer choices A and B. To set up an equation, label the percent of white chocolate as x:

$$5x + 3(1-x) = 4.20$$

$$5x + 3 - 3x = 4.20$$

$$2x = 1.20$$

$$x = .6$$

7. Which of the following equations represents a line passing through $(-3, 4)$ and $(-5, 2)$?

   A. $x - y = -7$

   B. $-3x + 4y = 25$

   C. $-2x + 4y = 18$

   D. $2y - 5x = 29$

7. The correct answer is A. To find the proper equation, you have two options. First, you could determine the slope, y-intercept, and equation of the line. This will lead you to the correct answer, but is more timely, and unnecessary! Instead, use the two points given, and make sure they both fit into the answer choices. Answer choice A works for both points. Answer choice B works for $(-3, 4)$ but not $(-5, 2)$. Answer choices C and D work for only $(-5, 2)$.

8. Which of the following answer choices correctly factors $x^2 - 13x - 30$?

   A. $(x - 10)(x - 3)$

   B. $(x - 6)(x - 7)$

   C. $(x + 15)(x - 2)$

   D. $(x + 2)(x - 15)$

8. The correct answer is D. Think of the quadratic equation; the signs tell us that the negative number should be with the larger value (from the -13), and that a positive and a negative sign are involved (from the -30). Or you could just multiply out the answer choices—that's good practice!

9. Kathleen and Elizabeth jog a total of 23 miles today. If Kathleen jogs 5 more miles than Elizabeth, how many miles did Elizabeth jog?

A. 5

B. 9

C. 14

D. 16

9. Answer choice B is correct. Rather than write an algebraic equation, use the answer choices to your advantage. Start with one of the middle numbers— we'll start with B. If Elizabeth jogs 9 miles, then Kathleen jogs 5 more, or 14 total miles. Their total, 9 + 14, is 23, the amount the problem asks for.

10. Chris and Peter were the only two candidates for president of the school pre-medical club. If 416 votes were cast, and Chris received 38 more votes than Peter, how many votes did Peter receive?

A. 38

B. 189

C. 227

D. 378

10. Answer choice B is correct. This algebra question is best solved by Backsolving. Peter received fewer votes, so we know that he will receive less than half of the total votes. Eliminate C and D. Try B: If Peter received 189 votes, then Chris received 38 more, or 227. The total of 189 and 227 is 416— the amount we are looking for.

11. The solution of $|4x + 3| = 5$ is:

A. $-\dfrac{1}{2}$

B. $\dfrac{1}{2}$

C. 2

D. $\dfrac{1}{2}, -2$

11. The correct answer is D. To find the solution with an equation that includes absolute value, set up two equalities:

$$4x + 3 = -5 \quad \text{and} \quad 4x + 3 = 5$$

$$x = -2 \qquad\qquad x = \dfrac{1}{2}$$

12. If $\dfrac{2x-5}{3} = \dfrac{x+7}{2}$, then $x =$

   A. 5

   B. 7

   C. 17

   D. 31

12. The correct answer is D. To find the value of x, use the method of cross-multiplication. After cross-multiplying, you will have

$$4x - 10 = 3x + 21$$

Next, solve for x:

$$x = 31$$

13. What is the perimeter of a triangle with lengths $(3x - 4)$, $(2x + 9)$, and $(8 - 2x)$?

   A. $7x + 21$

   B. $7x + 13$

   C. $3x + 21$

   D. $3x + 13$

13. The correct answer is D. To find the perimeter of a triangle, sum the values of all the lengths of the triangle. Here we have:

$$(3x - 4) + (2x + 9) + (8 - 2x) =$$
$$3x + 2x - 2x - 4 + 9 + 8 = 3x + 13$$

14. Which of the following lines is perpendicular to the line $3y = 9x + 3$?

   A. $6y + 2x = 6$

   B. $6y = 18x + 6$

   C. $3y = 3x + 9$

   D. $10y + 2x = 12$

14. The correct answer is A. Remember the rule for perpendicular lines: Two lines are perpendicular if the product of their slopes is -1. Start by finding the slope of the given line:

$$3y = 9x + 3$$

Divide by 3 to get the equation in proper $y = mx + b$ form:

$$y = 3x + 1$$

So the slope is 3. A perpendicular line will have a slope of $-\dfrac{1}{3}$. Answer choice A has this slope.

15. The total area of a figure is $8b^2 - b + 8$. There are three regions to the figure: Region I has area of $4b^2 + 5b + 2$. Region II has area of $b^2 + b - 3$. What is the area of Region III?

A. $3b^2 - 7b + 9$

B. $3b^2 - 5b + 7$

C. $3b^2 - 7b + 3$

D. $\dfrac{8}{5}b^2 - \dfrac{1}{6}b + 8$

15. The correct answer is A. Sum the values of Region I and Region II to get $5b^2 + 6b - 1$. Now subtract this from the total of $8b^2 - b + 8$ to get the value for Region III.

16. Tim roles a die and gets a three. What is the probability that the next throw will NOT be a three?

A. 1

B. $\dfrac{5}{6}$

C. $\dfrac{1}{2}$

D. $\dfrac{1}{3}$

16. Answer choice B is correct. There are six numbers on a die: 1, 2, 3, 4, 5, and 6. There are six possible outcomes, and we are looking for 5 possible outcomes (a role of 1, 2, 4, 5, or 6 is a "not three").

Therefore, the probability is $\dfrac{5}{6}$. Remember, Tim's first throw has nothing to do with his second throw.

17. A line passes through the following points: $(5, -2)$, $(-1, -6)$, and $(4, k)$. What is the value of k?

A. -4

B. $\dfrac{2}{3}$

C. $\dfrac{3}{2}$

D. $-\dfrac{8}{3}$

17. The correct answer is D. First, find the slope of the line with the two points that are given: $\dfrac{[-6 - (-2)]}{[-1 - 5]} = \dfrac{-4}{-6} = \dfrac{2}{3}$

With the slope of $\dfrac{2}{3}$, use this and another point to find the value of k:

$$\dfrac{2}{3} = \dfrac{(k + 6)}{[4 - (-1)]}$$

$$\dfrac{2}{3} = \dfrac{(k + 6)}{5}$$

$$10 = 3k + 18$$

$$-3k = 8$$

$$k = -\dfrac{8}{3}$$

18. What is the value of y if $\sqrt{y+6} = 8$?

    A. 2

    B. 10

    C. $\dfrac{8}{3}$

    D. 58

18. The correct answer is D. To find the value of y, square both sides of each equation:

$$y + 6 = 64$$

Remember that

$$\sqrt{(y+6)^2} = y + 6, \text{ and } y = 58$$

19. If (x, y) is the solution of the system of equations $\{x - 2y = 9, 2x + y = 8\}$, then the value of $x + y$ is:

    A. 3

    B. 5

    C. 8

    D. 16

19. The correct answer is A. To find the value of x and y, use the substitution method, as shown below:

$$x - 2y = 9$$

$$2x + y = 8$$

Multiply this equation by 2 to eliminate the y variable:

$$x - 2y = 9$$

$$4x + 2y = 16$$

Now sum the equations:

$$5x = 25$$

$$x = 5$$

Now that $x = 5$, substitute into either equation to find the value of y:

$$5 - 2y = 9$$

$$-2y = 4$$

$$y = -2$$

The sum of x and y is $5 + (-2) = 3$

20. The set of solution (s) to $5x^2 - 8x = -3$ is:

A. $\left(\dfrac{3}{5}, 1\right)$

B. 1

C. $-\dfrac{5}{3}$

D. –3

20. The correct answer is A. To solve this question, you need to know the quadratic equation. First, get the equation in standard form:

$$5x^2 - 8x + 3 = 0$$

then use the quadratic formula:

$$x = \frac{[-b \pm \sqrt{b^2 - 4ac}}{2a}$$

$$x = \frac{-(-8) \pm \sqrt{(-8)^2 - 4(5)(3)}}{2(5)}$$

$$x = \frac{8 \pm \sqrt{64 - 60}}{10}$$

$$x = \frac{8 \pm \sqrt{4}}{10}$$

$$x = \frac{8 \pm 2}{10}$$

$$x = \frac{10}{10}, \frac{6}{10}$$

$$x = 1, \frac{3}{5}$$

21. If x is a real number such that $0 < x < 3$, and $y = \dfrac{x^2}{2}$, then which of the following gives the complete range of the equation?

A. $0 < y < \dfrac{9}{2}$

B. $-\dfrac{2}{3} < y < 1$

C. $y < \dfrac{9}{2}$

D. $y > 0$

21. The correct answer is A. To find the range of this function, try plugging in the extreme values for the domain. If we try $x = 0$, we get $y = 0$. If we try $x = 3$, we get $y = \dfrac{9}{2}$. Therefore, the values for y must be between 0 and $\dfrac{9}{2}$. Answer choice A reflects this.

22. If $b = 5$, then find the value of $\dfrac{b^2 + b}{2b}$.

    A. 1.5

    B. 3

    C. 5

    D. 5.5

22. B is the correct answer. Start by substituting the value of 5 wherever you see b. Doing so will yield 30 in the numerator $(5 \times 5 + 5)$, and 10 in the denominator (2×5). The correct answer is $\dfrac{30}{10}$, or 3.

23. Simplify the following expression:

$$(3a^4b^5c^6d^{-2})^3$$

    A. $9a^7b^8c^9d$

    B. $9a^{12}b^{15}c^{18}d^{-6}$

    C. $27a^7b^8c^9d^6$

    D. $27a^{12}b^{15}c^{18}d^{-6}$

23. D is the correct answer. Here you are tested on your ability to work with exponents. Again, on these questions, use process of elimination to quickly navigate through. Starting with the coefficient, $3 \times 3 \times 3 = 27$; eliminate A and B. $(a^4)^3 = a^{12}$. Eliminate C. D is the correct answer.

24 and 25: For the questions below, use the following stem-and-leaf diagram:

Stem	Leaf
16	9
17	2, 8
18	3, 3, 3, 4, 6
19	0, 5, 6, 8, 9
20	1, 1, 3

24. The above stem-and-leaf diagram is a set of heights, in centimeters, of players on a high-school basketball team. What height shows up the most frequently?

    A. 3

    B. 18

    C. 183

    D. 201

24. C is the correct answer. The stem-and-leaf diagram shows us that the number 183 appears three times. No other number appears this frequently.

25. If you were to pick a number at random from the stem-and-leaf diagram above, what is the probability that the number would end in a 3?

A. $\frac{3}{18}$

B. $\frac{3}{16}$

C. $\frac{1}{4}$

D. $\frac{2}{5}$

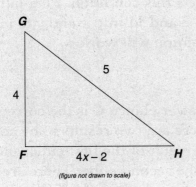
(figure not drawn to scale)

26. If the area of triangle *FGH* is 36, what is the value of *x*?

A. 5

B. 9

C. 12

D. 18

25. Answer choice C is correct. In order to find the probability, we need to find the total number of possible outcomes. If we count the numbers in the "leaf" section of the chart, we can see that there are 16 different possible outcomes. Four of these end in a 3. The probability is $\frac{4}{16}$, or $\frac{1}{4}$.

26. Answer choice A is correct. First, remember the formula for area of a triangle: $\frac{1}{2}bh$. If the area is 36, then base × height = 72. That means $4(4x - 2) = 72$. To solve this equation:

$$4x - 2 = 18$$

$$4x = 20$$

$$x = 5$$

27. When the factored polynomial $(x + 3)(x + 4)$ is expanded, the result is $x^2 + 7x + r$. What is the value of r?

A. 7

B. 12

C. 19

D. 24

28. Which of the following lines is parallel to the line represented by $y = -3x + 4$ and passes through point $(-3, 11)$?

A. $6x + 2y = -10$

B. $2y = -6x + 4$

C. $12x + 4y = 7$

D. $y = -3x + 11$

29. Marty has two numbered cubes, each numbered 1–6. What is the probability that when the cubes are tossed, the total will be an 8?

A. $\dfrac{1}{12}$

B. $\dfrac{5}{12}$

C. $\dfrac{5}{36}$

D. $\dfrac{1}{6}$

27. Answer choice B is the correct answer. Multiply the polynomial by using the foil method. Doing so yields $x^2 + 4x + 3x + 12$. The value of the coefficient is 12.

28. The correct answer is B. To be parallel, two lines must have the same slope. All of the equations in the answer choices have a slope of –3. But the question requires that the line pass also through point (–3, 11). Only answer choice B meets this condition. Plug in the values of –3 and 11 into x and y to test which equation will work.

29. Answer choice C is the correct answer. There are two results to be considered: the result of the first cube, and the result of the second cube. There are a total of six outcomes for the first cube: 1, 2, 3, 4, 5, and 6. The same is true for the second cube. If we were to combine every possible outcome, there are 36 different possibilities. Of these, 5 of them add up to 8:

2 and 6

3 and 5

4 and 4

5 and 3

6 and 2

30. The product of $\sqrt{2a}$ and $\sqrt{8a}$ is:

A. $4a$

B. $4a^2$

C. $16a$

D. $16a^2$

30. The correct answer is A. When multiplying with square roots, first put everything underneath one square root sign:

$$(2a)(8a) = \sqrt{16a^2}$$

The square root of this combined term is $4a$.

ANSWERS AND EXPLANATIONS FOR SESSION TWO

Grid-In Answer Key

1. 12
2. 10
3. 16
4. 28
5. 1
6. 7
7. $\frac{1}{4}$, or .25
8. 10.8
9. $\frac{3}{2}$
10. 9

Grid-In Explanations

1. The correct answer is 12. Use the following chart to help determine how to find the answer:

	Rate	Time	Distance
First Part Trip	35 mph	4	(35)(4) = 140 miles
Second Part Trip	55 mph	x	55x
Total Trip	50 mph	4 + x	200 + 50x

This creates the equation

$$140 + 55x = 200 + 50x$$

$$5x = 60$$

$$x = 12$$

2. The correct answer is 10. Factor the equation to set up the solutions for x:

$$2x^2 - 14x + 20 = 0$$

$$(2x - 4)(x - 5) = 0$$

$$2x - 4 = 0 \qquad x - 5 = 0$$

$$x = 2 \qquad x = 5$$

The product of the solutions, 2 and 5, is 10.

3. The correct answer is 16. To find this answer, sum the values of the angles in the triangle:

$$3y - 6 + 2y + 7 + 6y + 3 = 180$$

$$11y + 4 = 180$$

$$11y = 176$$

$$y = 16$$

4. The correct answer is 28. To find the correct answer, we need to set up a system. To start with, let t = # of tools bought originally.

We know that first, half of these tools $\left(\dfrac{1}{2}\right)$ are given away, and then five more are given away, so 9 are left. To summarize:

$$t - \frac{1}{2}t - 5 = 9$$

$$\frac{1}{2}t = 14$$

$$t = 28$$

5. The correct answer is 1. To find the correct answer, substitute the value of x and y into the equation:

$$(3)^2 - 2(3)(2) + (2)^2 =$$

$$9 - 12 + 4 = 1$$

6. The correct answer is 7. To find the value of k, factor the polynomial, as follows:

$$t^2 + 2t - 35 =$$

$$(t + \quad)(t - \quad) =$$

$$(t + 7)(t - 5)$$

Therefore, k is 7.

7. The correct answer is $\frac{1}{4}$, or .25. To solve this equation, combine like terms:

$$\frac{2}{\partial} = 8$$

$$2 = 8\partial$$

$$\frac{2}{8} = \partial$$

$$\partial = \frac{1}{4}$$

8. The correct answer is 10.8. This is a proportion question. To set up your equation, make a fraction of the two unrelated terms:

$$\frac{1 \text{ in.}}{3 \text{ ft.}} = \frac{3.6 \text{ in.}}{x \text{ ft.}}$$

Cross multiply to solve for x:

$$x = (3)(3.6)$$

$$x = 10.8$$

9. The correct answer is $\frac{3}{2}$. To find the slope of a line, make sure the equation is in the proper $y = mx + b$ format:

$$y = mx + b$$

$$-4y = -6x - 11$$

$$y = \frac{3}{2}x + \frac{11}{4}$$

The slope is $\frac{3}{2}$. Parallel lines have the same slope, so the correct answer is $\frac{3}{2}$.

10. The correct answer is 9. A key to this question is the word *exactly*. Because the question requires her to pay exactly $1.95, she cannot go over that total. While 8 quarters would equal 2 dollars, it does not give us an exact total. *7* quarters and 2 dimes must be spent in order to get exactly $1.95.

Written Response Explanation

In order to receive full credit for the problem, be sure to clearly label and identify your work.

1. First you need to create equations for the information given in the problem:

$$\text{Let } x = \text{year of work for Job I}$$

$$\text{Let } y = \text{year of work for Job II}$$

Job I: Yearly Income = $30,000 + $3,000(x − 1)

Job II: Yearly Income = $37,000 + $2,000(y − 1)

2. To find the amount of money made during Year 3, plug into the equations:

Job I: $30,000 + $3,000(3 − 1) =

$30,000 + $3,000(2) =

$36,000 =

Job II: $37,000 + $2,000(3 − 1) =

$37,000 + $2,000(2) =

$41,000

3. To find out which job will pay more money during Year 5, do the same as you did in step 2. Clearly label and summarize your findings:

Job I: $30,000 + $3,000(5 − 1) =

$30,000 + $3,000(4) =

$42,000

Job II: $37,000 + $2,000(5 − 1) =

$37,000 + $2,000(4) =

$45,000

As shown above, Job II would pay the graduate more money during Year 5.

4. To find out which job will pay more during the tenth year, do the exact same thing as in step 3. Again, label clearly:

Job I: $30,000 + $3,000(10 − 1) =

                        $30,000 + $3,000(9) =

                        $57,000

Job II: $37,000 + $2,000(10 − 1) =

                        $37,000 + $2,000(9) =

                        $55,000

As shown above, Job I would pay the graduate more money during year 10.

5. Finally, you want to find the year in which the two jobs will pay the same amount of money. If you aren't sure how to complete this step, use the information you've found from above. The year should be somewhere between Year 5 and Year 10, because during these years Job I becomes a higher-paying job than Job II.

So you're looking to see when the yearly salary will be equal, or, in our problem above, when $x = y$. An equation could look like this:

$$\$30{,}000 + \$3{,}000(x − 1) = \$37{,}000 + \$2{,}000(y − 1)$$

Here $x = y$, so we can just label all variables as x:

$$\$30{,}000 + \$3{,}000x − 3{,}000 = \$37{,}000 + \$2{,}000x - \$2{,}000$$

$$\$27{,}000 + \$3{,}000x = \$35{,}000 + \$2{,}000x$$

$$\$1{,}000x = \$8{,}000$$

$$x = 8$$

In Year 8, the two jobs will pay the same amount of money.

THE PRINCETON REVIEW
ALGEBRA GSE
PRACTICE TEST II

11. 9^9 is how many times greater than 3^6?

  A. 3^3

  B. 3^{12}

  C. 3^{15}

  D. 6^3

12. Translate the following sentences into an equation: Rob got a total of 22 hits during baseball season. That was three more than twice as many hits as Clint got. How many hits did Clint get during the baseball season?

  A. $22 = 3 + 2x$

  B. $22 - 3x = 2x$

  C. $2(22 + 3) = x$

  D. $22 + 3 + 2x$

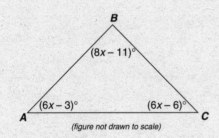
(figure not drawn to scale)

13. Triangle *ABC* has angles with the indicated measures. The order of the angles, from smallest to largest is as follows:

  A. *A, B, C*

  B. *B, A, C*

  C. *C, B, A*

  D. *C, A, B*

14. Two cars are traveling down the highway at different speeds. If one of them travels 180 km and the other travels 150 km, what is the difference in their speed, in km/h, if they both travel for 2 hours?

  A. 90

  B. 75

  C. 30

  D. 15

15. When the factored polynomial $(3a + b)(-2a - 4b)$ is multiplied, the solution is $-6a^2 - 4b^2 - 28$. What is the value of ab?

  A. -28

  B. -14

  C. 2

  D. 14

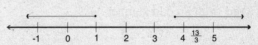

16. Which of the following represents the graph above?

  A. $3x - 8 = 5$

  B. $|3x + 8| = 5$

  C. $3x - 8 \geq -5$

  D. $|3x - 8| \geq 5$

17. If $4(2x + 1) = 3(x + 13)$, what is the value of x?

  A. $\dfrac{35}{11}$

  B. 7

  C. $\dfrac{43}{5}$

  D. 12

18. Which of the following lines is perpendicular to $y = -2x + 4$?

    A. $4y = 3x + 12$

    B. $-3x + 4y = 2$

    C. $4y = -12x + 16$

    D. $2y - x = 2$

19. If y is the quotient of $\dfrac{x^2 + 5x + 6}{x + 2}$, then what is the value of y?

    A. $x + 3$

    B. $x + 7$

    C. $2x + 3$

    D. $2x + 7$

20. A card is drawn from a standard deck of cards. What is the probability that that card is red, with an odd number?

    A. $\dfrac{1}{2}$

    B. $\dfrac{4}{13}$

    C. $\dfrac{5}{13}$

    D. $\dfrac{2}{13}$

21. A line with slope of 2 passes through points $(4, 2)$ and $(a, 6)$. What is the value of a?

    A. 2

    B. 4

    C. 6

    D. 8

22. What is the value of x if $\sqrt{2x - 5} = 7$?

    A. 6

    B. 12

    C. 27

    D. 54

23. If (x, y) is the solution of the system of equations $\{4x - y = 5, 2x + y = 13\}$, then the value of xy is:

    A. 3

    B. 7

    C. 10

    D. 21

24. The product of x and y is 21. What is the solution set to the equation $4 + x^2 = 2x^2 - 5$?

    A. $x = 3$

    B. $x = -3$

    C. $x = -3, 3$

    D. $x = 1$

25. Solve for a: $6(3a - 2) + 5a = 57$

    A. 1

    B. 2

    C. 3

    D. 4

26. A line has a slope of $\dfrac{2}{3}$ and passes through points $(2, 6)$ and $(5, k)$. What is the value of k?

    A. -8

    B. -2

    C. 2

    D. 8

27. Forty-two people have registered for the raffle. If there are twice as many children as adults signed up, how many children are registered for the raffle?

   A. 14

   B. 18

   C. 20

   D. 28

28. If the perimeter of a triangle is $8y - 18$, and two of the sides of the triangle are $(5y - 8)$ and $(7y - 3)$, what is the third side of the triangle?

   A. $-4y + 7$

   B. $-4y - 7$

   C. $6y + 3$

   D. $2y - 9$

29. If $c = 3$, and d is twice the value of c, then what is the value of $\dfrac{dc^2 - 2cd}{2cd}$?

   A. .5

   B. 2

   C. 18

   D. 36

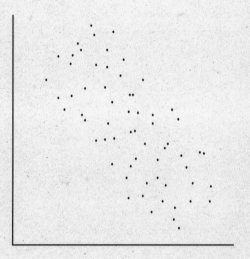

30. Looking at the scatter plot above, what type of relationship exists between the variables in each graph?

   A. Positive relationship

   B. Negative relationship

   C. No relationship

   D. Circular relationship

1

YOUR NAME: _____
(Print)
　　　　　　　Last　　　　　　　　　　First　　　　　　　　　　M.I.

SIGNATURE: _____ **DATE:** ____ / ____ / ____

HOME ADDRESS: _____
(Print)
　　　　　　　　　　　　Number and Street

_____
　　　　City　　　　　　　　　State　　　　　　　　Zip Code

PHONE NO.: _____
(Print)

Completely darken bubbles with a No. 2 pencil. If you make a mistake, be sure to erase mark completely. Erase all stray marks.

Practice Test II

1. Ⓐ Ⓑ Ⓒ Ⓓ　　16. Ⓐ Ⓑ Ⓒ Ⓓ
2. Ⓐ Ⓑ Ⓒ Ⓓ　　17. Ⓐ Ⓑ Ⓒ Ⓓ
3. Ⓐ Ⓑ Ⓒ Ⓓ　　18. Ⓐ Ⓑ Ⓒ Ⓓ
4. Ⓐ Ⓑ Ⓒ Ⓓ　　19. Ⓐ Ⓑ Ⓒ Ⓓ
5. Ⓐ Ⓑ Ⓒ Ⓓ　　20. Ⓐ Ⓑ Ⓒ Ⓓ
6. Ⓐ Ⓑ Ⓒ Ⓓ　　21. Ⓐ Ⓑ Ⓒ Ⓓ
7. Ⓐ Ⓑ Ⓒ Ⓓ　　22. Ⓐ Ⓑ Ⓒ Ⓓ
8. Ⓐ Ⓑ Ⓒ Ⓓ　　23. Ⓐ Ⓑ Ⓒ Ⓓ
9. Ⓐ Ⓑ Ⓒ Ⓓ　　24. Ⓐ Ⓑ Ⓒ Ⓓ
10. Ⓐ Ⓑ Ⓒ Ⓓ　　25. Ⓐ Ⓑ Ⓒ Ⓓ
11. Ⓐ Ⓑ Ⓒ Ⓓ　　26. Ⓐ Ⓑ Ⓒ Ⓓ
12. Ⓐ Ⓑ Ⓒ Ⓓ　　27. Ⓐ Ⓑ Ⓒ Ⓓ
13. Ⓐ Ⓑ Ⓒ Ⓓ　　28. Ⓐ Ⓑ Ⓒ Ⓓ
14. Ⓐ Ⓑ Ⓒ Ⓓ　　29. Ⓐ Ⓑ Ⓒ Ⓓ
15. Ⓐ Ⓑ Ⓒ Ⓓ　　30. Ⓐ Ⓑ Ⓒ Ⓓ

SESSION TWO

Directions

The following questions are similar to the multiple-choice questions, but answer choices are not provided. You must determine the answers yourself using separate scratch paper, and then use a special area on the answer sheet like the one on page 195 to bubble in your answers. If the answer is a mixed numeral, it is to be gridded as a decimal or improper fraction (e.g., $3\frac{1}{2}$ should be gridded as $\frac{7}{2}$ or 3.5).

Grid-In Questions

1. What is the perimeter of the triangle with vertices (4, 7), (4, 15), and (10, 7)?

2. A line with a slope of $\frac{4}{7}$ is represented by the equation $14y - kx = -11$. What is the value of k?

3. The total area of a triangle is divided into three regions. The total area is $4a^2 + 2a + 8$. If the area of Region I is $a^2 + 5a$, the Region of Area II is $2a^2 + 3$, and $a = 3$, what is the area of Region III?

4. Ben has two numbered cubes, each with sides labeled 1, 2, 3, 4, 5, and 6. When the cubes are tossed, what is the probability that Ben throws two sides that total 11?

5. A line passes through points (3, 8), (1, 4), and (–1, a). What is the value of a?

6. Solve the following equation and give the answer to the nearest hundredth:
$$10x + 4 = 34 - 6(x - 14)$$

7. What is the value of $\sqrt{8x+8} + \sqrt{2x+2}$ if $x = 1$?

8. If $2x + 3y = 11$ and $5y - x = 1$, what is the value of y?

9. The product of all real-number solutions for x in the equation $20x^2 - 15x = 0$ is:

10. If $\frac{3x-5}{4} = \frac{5-x}{5}$, then the value of x, rounded to the nearest tenth is:

Written Response Question

The school board is looking to hire additional faculty members. They can hire both teachers and aides. The board has determined that a minimum of 20 faculty members must be hired, including at least 12 teachers. To create an adequate balance, the number of aides must be no more than twice the number of teachers.

Given this information:

1. Write an inequality for each condition given in the information above.

2. Graph the inequalities on the same coordinate axis. Be sure to shade the appropriate region on the graph, and label the graph clearly.

3. Imagine that the school board hires 10 teachers and 22 aides. Will all of the conditions be satisfied? Why or why not?

GRID-IN ANSWER SHEET

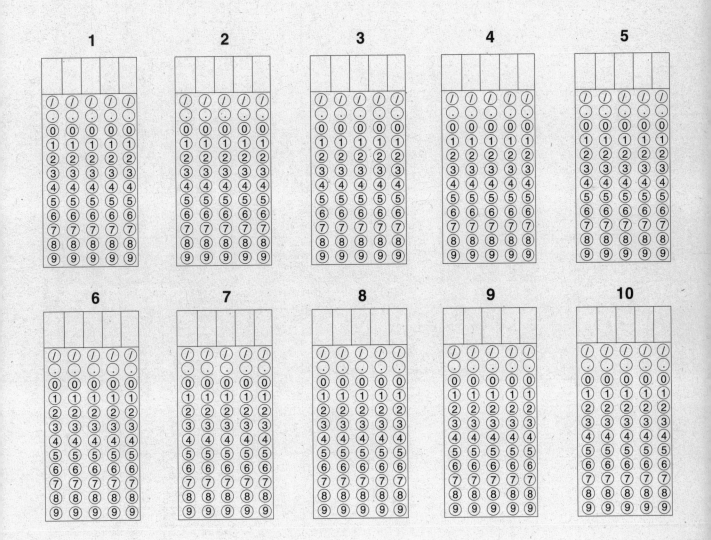

WRITTEN RESPONSE
ANSWER SHEET

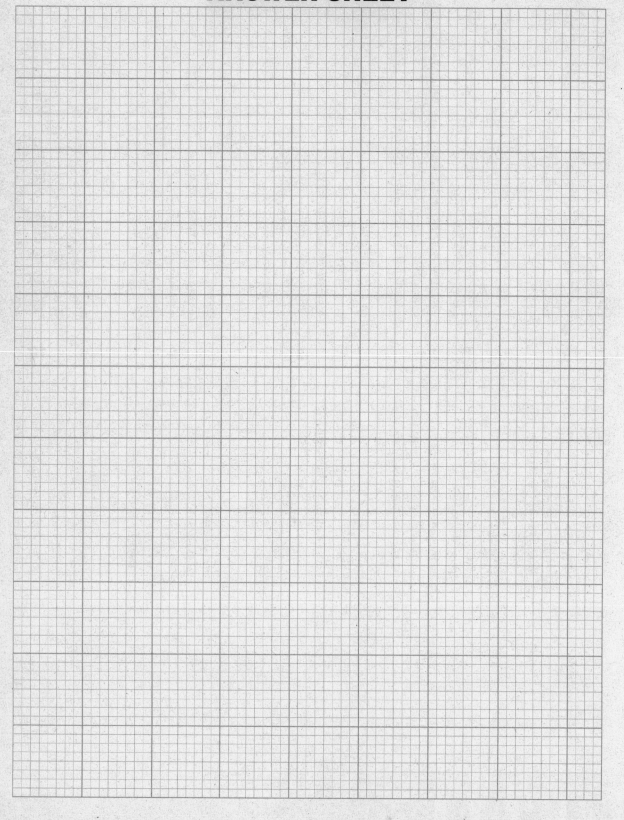

ANSWERS AND EXPLANATIONS FOR SESSION ONE

Answer Key

1.	D	11.	B	21.	C
2.	B	12.	A	22.	C
3.	C	13.	D	23.	D
4.	D	14.	D	24.	C
5.	B	15.	C	25.	C
6.	C	16.	D	26.	D
7.	A	17.	B	27.	D
8.	B	18.	D	28.	B
9.	C	19.	A	29.	A
10.	C	20.	D	30.	B

Explanations

1. The value of cents of $(18z + 4)$ nickels is:

   A. $18z + 20$

   B. $4z + 90$

   C. $90z + 4$

   D. $90z + 20$

1. Answer choice D is correct. This question asks you to take an algebraic expression and change it to express a different set of units. Here, the expression is originally in nickels, which is five times the value of cents (there are five nickels for one cent). To change the expression, multiply the entire expression by 5: $(18z + 4)5 = 90z + 20$.

2. A cube numbered 1 through 6 is tossed. What is the probability that either a 1 or a 6 will be rolled?

A. $\frac{1}{6}$

B. $\frac{1}{3}$

C. $\frac{1}{2}$

D. $\frac{2}{3}$

2. The correct answer is B. There are six total outcomes, and two events that we are looking for. Thus, the probability is $\frac{2}{6}$, or $\frac{1}{3}$.

3. The number of real-number solutions to $3x^2 = 7 - 2x$ is:

A. 0

B. 1

C. 2

D. Infinitely many solutions

3. The correct answer is C. In order to find how many real-number solutions exist for an equation, you need to evaluate part of the quadratic formula, known as the discriminant. The discriminant is defined as the number underneath the square root sign in the quadratic formula, $b^2 - 4ac$. So first get the equation in proper form:

$$3x^2 + 2x - 7 = 0$$

and $a = 3$, $b = 2$, and $c = -7$

$$b^2 - 4ac = (2)^2 - 4(3)(-7) = 4 + 84 = 88$$

A positive value for the discriminant indicates that there are two solutions.

4. The lines $3x - y = -5$ and $5y - zx = 10$ are parallel. What is the value of z?

   A. -15

   B. 3

   C. 10

   D. 15

4. The correct answer is D. First find the slope of the line:

$$3x - y = -5$$

$$3x + 5 = y \quad \text{or} \quad y = 3x + 5$$

Both the two lines must have a slope of 3 since they are parallel. Now you can use this to determine z:

$$5y - zx = 10$$

$$5y = zx + 10$$

$$y = \frac{z}{5}x + 2$$

If the slope equals three, then $\frac{z}{5} = 3$.

$z = 15$.

5. If $\dfrac{4y - 2}{2} = \dfrac{y + 6}{3}$ then $y =$

   A. $\dfrac{5}{9}$

   B. $\dfrac{9}{5}$

   C. 10

   D. 18

5. The correct answer is B. To find the value of y, use the method of cross-multiplication. The calculations should look like this:

$$3(4y - 2) = 2(y + 6)$$

$$12y - 6 = 2y + 12$$

$$10y = 18$$

$$y = \frac{18}{10}, \text{ or } \frac{9}{5}$$

6. Shon likes to take pens from other employees in his office. He currently has 12 more pens than the rest of the office has, combined. If there are 84 pens in the office, how many does Shon currently have?

   A. 12

   B. 36

   C. 48

   D. 72

6. The correct answer is C. If Shon has more than the rest of the office, we know that he will have over half of the pens—eliminate answer choices A and B. Backsolve using answer choice C: If Shon has 48 pens, then the office has 12 fewer, or 36 pens. The total of 48 and 36 is 84—the number given in the equation.

7. Given the equation $x^2 - 4x - 7 = 0$, what value needs to be added in order to complete the square?

   A. 4

   B. 7

   C. 11

   D. 18

7. The correct answer is A. In order to complete the square, we need to first isolate the constant:

   $$x^2 - 4x = 7$$

   Then we need to add 4 in order to create a perfect square:

   $$x^2 - 4x + 4 = 7 + 4$$

   $$(x - 2)(x - 2) = 11$$

8. What is the value of y in a triangle where the angles measure $(5y + 16)$, $(6y - 16)$, and $(8y - 10)$?

   A. 5

   B. 10

   C. 16

   D. 20

8. The correct answer is B. The sum of the angles in a triangle add up to 180. After summing the angles, the total becomes:

   $$19y - 10 = 180$$

   $$19y = 190$$

   $$y = 10$$

9. Suppose that the value s is the total amount of tickets sold to the dance. If each of the sixth, seven, and eighth grades sold the same number of tickets, write an expression for the number of tickets sold by each grade:

    A. $6s + 7s + 8s$

    B. $6s(1 + s + 2s)$

    C. $\dfrac{s}{3}$

    D. $\dfrac{s}{7}$

9. C is the correct answer. s is the total number of tickets sold. If we want to find the number of tickets for one class, we could set up the following expression: Total = # tickets sold by 6th grade + # tickets sold by 7th grade + # tickets sold by 8th grade. Now, you're told that the number sold by each grade is equal, so you can summarize the equation:

    $$\text{Total} = 3 \times \text{Number sold by a grade}$$

    $$s = 3 \times \text{Number sold by a grade}$$

    $$\frac{s}{3} = \text{Number sold by a grade}$$

10. Simplify the following expression:

    A. a^4b^8

    B. a^2b^4

    C. ab^2

    D. a^8b^{10}

10. The correct answer is C. Start by ignoring the square root sign and simplifying the term. Use the rules of exponents to simplify. To divide exponents, subtract them. The simplified value is a^2b^4. The square root of this value is ab^2.

11. 9^9 is how many times greater than 3^6?

    A. 3^3

    B. 3^{12}

    C. 3^{15}

    D. 6^3

11. B is the correct answer. Can we manipulate these numbers? Remember that you need to have the same base in order to combine and simplify exponents. Is there any way to get these two numbers to have the same base? Yes! What do 9 and 3 have in common? Both are multiples of 3. Try rewriting the first number with 3 as the base:

    $$9^9 = (3^2)^9 = 3^{18}$$

    Now, we can divide: $\dfrac{3^{18}}{3^6} = 3^{12}$.

12. Translate the following sentences into an equation: Rob got a total of 22 hits during baseball season. That was three more than twice as many hits as Clint got. How many hits did Clint get during the baseball season?

A. $22 = 3 + 2x$

B. $22 - 3x = 2x$

C. $2(22 + 3) = x$

D. $22 + 3 + 2x$

12. Answer choice A is correct. Translate the statement you're given into its mathematical equivalents. We're told that 22 was (=) 3 more than (3 +) twice as many hits as Clint got (2 × *our unknown*, or $2x$). If we put this all together, we get $22 = 3 + 2x$.

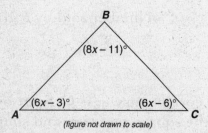
(figure not drawn to scale)

13. Triangle *ABC* has angles with the indicated measures. The order of the angles, from smallest to largest is as follows:

A. *A, B, C*

B. *B, A, C*

C. *C, B, A*

D. *C, A, B*

13. D is the correct answer. To determine the order of the angles, first solve for the variable x.

$(6x - 3) + (6x - 6) + (8x - 11) = 180.$

$$20x - 20 = 180$$

$$20x = 200$$

$$x = 10$$

Now substitute back into the equation in order to calculate the sizes of the angles: The *largest* angle is angle *B* (69), followed by angle *A* (57), then by angle *C* (54). From *smallest* to *largest*, the order is *C, A, B*. Be careful that you do not select answer choice B, which orders the angles from largest to smallest.

14. Two cars are traveling down the highway at different speeds. If one of them travels 180 km and the other travels 150 km, what is the difference in their speed, in km/h, if they both travel for 2 hours?

A. 90

B. 75

C. 30

D. 15

14. Answer choice D is correct. After two hours, the two cars are 30 km apart (180 − 150). 30 km, divided by 2 hours $= \dfrac{30}{2}$, or 15 km/h.

15. When the factored polynomial $(3a + b)(-2a - 4b)$ is multiplied, the solution is $-6a^2 - 4b^2 - 28$. What is the value of ab?

A. −28

B. −14

C. 2

D. 14

15. Answer choice C is correct. Use FOIL to expand the term:
$$(3a + b)(-2a - 4b) =$$
$$-6a^2 - 12ab - 2ab - 4b^2$$

Now combine the middle terms to get: $-14ab$. In the problem above, the equation is written as −28, so $ab = 2$.

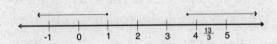

16. Which of the following represents the graph above?

A. $3x - 8 = 5$

B. $|3x + 8| = 5$

C. $3x - 8 \geq -5$

D. $|3x - 8| \geq 5$

16. The correct answer is D. We can eliminate answer choice A—it represents only one point. Answer choice B represents two points. Answer choice C represents the equation $x \geq 1$. By POE, we have answer choice D.

17. If $4(2x + 1) = 3(x + 13)$, what is the value of x?

A. $\dfrac{35}{11}$

B. 7

C. $\dfrac{43}{5}$

D. 12

17. Answer choice B is the correct answer. Find the value of x as follows:
$$8x + 4 = 3x + 39$$
$$5x = 35$$
$$x = 7$$

18. Which of the following lines is perpendicular to
    $y = -2x + 4$?

    A. $4y = 3x + 12$

    B. $-3x + 4y = 2$

    C. $4y = -12x + 16$

    D. $2y - x = 2$

18. The correct answer is D. Remember the rule for perpendicular lines: Two lines are perpendicular if the product of their slopes is −1. Start by finding the slope of the line given:

$$y = -2x + 4$$

This equation is in proper $y = mx + b$ form, and the slope is −2. A line perpendicular to this line will have a slope of $\frac{1}{2}$, and answer choice D has this slope.

If you rearrange the equation in choice D, you will get:

$$2y = x + 2; \quad y = \frac{1}{2}x + 1$$

19. If y is the quotient of $\dfrac{(x^2 + 5x + 6)}{(x + 2)}$, then what is the value of y?

    A. $x + 3$

    B. $x + 7$

    C. $2x + 3$

    D. $2x + 7$

19. Answer choice A is the correct answer. This is a simple factoring problem:

$(x^2 + 5x + 6)$ factors to $(x + 3)(x + 2)$, so

$$\frac{(x + 3)(x + 2)}{(x + 2)} \text{ and the } (x + 2)\text{s}$$

cancel out to give you answer choice A, $x + 3$.

20. A card is drawn from a standard deck of cards. What is the probability that that card is red, with an odd number?

    A. $\dfrac{1}{2}$

    B. $\dfrac{4}{13}$

    C. $\dfrac{5}{13}$

    D. $\dfrac{2}{13}$

20. Answer choice D is correct. There are four odd cards in a suit and four suits, so $4(4) = 16 \div 52$ (total number of cards) equals the chances of getting an odd card, multiplied by $\dfrac{1}{2}$, which is the chance of getting a red card, so

$$\left(\frac{16}{52}\right)\left(\frac{1}{2}\right) = \frac{8}{52} = \frac{4}{26} = \frac{2}{13}$$

21. A line with slope of 2 passes through points $(4, 2)$ and $(a, 6)$. What is the value of a?

    A. 2

    B. 4

    C. 6

    D. 8

21. The correct answer is C. With a slope of 2, we can use the difference of two points to find the value of a:

$$2 = \frac{6 - 2}{a - 4}$$
$$2 = \frac{4}{a - 4}$$
$$2a - 8 = 4$$
$$2a = 12$$
$$a = 6$$

22. What is the value of x if $\sqrt{2x - 5} = 7$?

    A. 6

    B. 12

    C. 27

    D. 54

22. The correct answer is C. To find the value of x, square both sides of each equation to get:

$$2x - 5 = 49$$

and then solve for x:

$$2x = 54$$
$$x = 27$$

23. If (x, y) is the solution of the system of equations $\{4x - y = 5, 2x + y = 13\}$, then the value of xy is:

A. 3

B. 7

C. 10

D. 21

23. The correct answer is D. To find the value of xy, we first need to solve the system of equations for both x and y. To do so, use the substitution method, as demonstrated below:

$$4x - y = 5$$

$$2x + y = 13$$

Now add the two equations together to eliminate the y variable:

$$6x = 18$$

$$x = 3$$

Now that you have x, solve for y by placing the value of x into either equation:

$$4x - y = 5$$

$$4(3) - y = 5$$

$$12 - y = 5$$

$$-y = -7$$

$$y = 7$$

and $xy = (3)(7) = 21$

24. The product of x and y is 21. What is the solution set to the equation $4 + x^2 = 2x^2 - 5$?

A. $x = 3$

B. $x = -3$

C. $x = -3, 3$

D. $x = 1$

24. The correct answer is C. To find the value of x, solve the equation by isolating the variables, as follows:

$$4 = x^2 - 5$$

$$9 = x^2$$

$$3 = x$$

25. Solve for a: $6(3a - 2) + 5a = 57$

    A. 1

    B. 2

    C. 3

    D. 4

25. C is the correct answer. The solution is:

$$18a - 12 + 5a = 57$$

$$23a - 12 = 57$$

$$23a = 69$$

$$a = 3$$

26. A line has a slope of $\frac{2}{3}$ and passes through points $(2, 6)$ and $(5, k)$. What is the value of k?

    A. −8

    B. −2

    C. 2

    D. 8

26. Answer choice D is the correct answer. Set up the slope equation by using the difference between two points:

$$\text{Slope} = \frac{2}{3} = \frac{k - 6}{5 - 2}$$

$$= \frac{2}{3} = \frac{k - 6}{3}$$

Since the denominators are the same, we can disregard the denominator and solve:

$$2 = k - 6$$

$$8 = k$$

27. Forty-two people have registered for the raffle. If there are twice as many children as adults signed up, how many children are registered for the raffle?

    A. 14

    B. 18

    C. 20

    D. 28

27. The correct answer is D. You can Backsolve to solve this problem rather than writing an algebraic expression. First, you know that there are more children than adults, and you can therefore eliminate all answer choices but D! To solve the problem, let's look at answer choice D: if there are 28 children, then there are half as many adults, so there are 14 adults. The total number of children plus the number of adults is equal to $28 + 14 = 42$; the number that the question asks for.

28. If the perimeter of a triangle is $8y - 18$, and two of the sides of the triangle are $(5y - 8)$ and $(7y - 3)$, what is the third side of the triangle?

A. $-4y + 7$

B. $-4y - 7$

C. $6y + 3$

D. $2y - 9$

28. The correct answer is B. To find the third side of the triangle, sum the first two sides of the triangle:

$$(5y - 8) + (7y - 3) = 12y - 11$$

$$(12y - 11) + (3rd\ Side) = 8y - 18$$

$$4y + (3rd\ Side) = -7$$

$$3rd\ Side = -4y - 7$$

29. If $c = 3$, and d is twice the value of c, then what is the value of $\dfrac{dc^2 - 2cd}{2cd}$?

A. $.5$

B. 2

C. 18

D. 36

29. The answer is A. First, we need to find the value of d. The value of the variable is twice the value of the variable c; $c = 3$, so $d = 6$. Now that you have the value for each variable, plug these numbers into the expression:

$$\frac{6 \cdot 3^2 - 2 \cdot 3 \cdot 6}{2 \cdot 3 \cdot 6}$$

$$= \frac{6 \cdot 9 - 36}{36}$$

$$= \frac{54 - 36}{36} = \frac{18}{36} = \frac{1}{2}$$

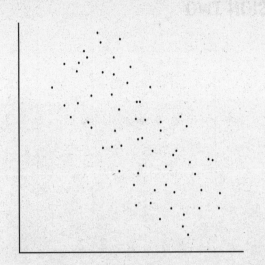

30. Looking at the scatter plot above, what type of relationship exists between the variables in each graph?

    A. Positive relationship

    B. Negative relationship

    C. No relationship

    D. Circular relationship

30. Choice B is correct. In order to determine a relationship demonstrated by scattergrams, remember to draw the line of best fit. Here, the line of best fit indicates a negative relationship between the two variables, and B is the correct answer.

ANSWERS AND EXPLANATIONS FOR SESSION TWO

Grid-In Answer Key

1. 24
2. 8
3. 5
4. $\dfrac{1}{8}$ or .0556
5. 0
6. 7.13
7. 6
8. 1
9. 0
10. 2.4

Grid-In Explanations

1. The answer is 24. To find the perimeter, map out the triangle. When you plot the points of the triangle, you will see that it is a right triangle, with leg lengths of 6 and 8. The third side of this triangle must be 10 (it is a 6-8-10 triangle). The sum of the lengths: 6, 8, and 10, is 24.

2. The correct answer is 8. To find the value of k, set up the equation in slope-intercept form:

$$y = mx + b$$

$$14y - kx = -11$$

$$14y = kx - 11$$

$$y = \frac{kx}{14} - \frac{11}{14}$$

We know that the slope value, or m is $\dfrac{kx}{14}$. If the slope is $\dfrac{4}{7}$, then $k = 8$.

3.   The correct answer is 5. First find the area of Region III by adding algebraic expressions for Regions I and II, and subtracting that total from the overall area of the triangle.

$$4a^2 + 2a + 8 = 2a^2 + 3 + a^2 + 5a + \text{(Region III)}$$

$$4a^2 + 2a + 8 = 3a^2 + 5a + 3 + \text{(Region III)}$$

$$a^2 - 3a + 5 = \text{Region III}.$$

Now that we know the equation the area for Region III, plug in the value of 3 for a to find the area of Region III:

$$(3)^2 - 3(3) + 5 =$$

$$9 - 9 + 5 =$$

$$5$$

4.   The correct answer is $\frac{2}{36}$, or $\frac{1}{8}$ (.0556 is also correct in decimal form). There are six possible outcomes from the first cube, and six from the second cube. So there are 36 (6 times 6) possible outcomes when two cubes are tossed. To get an 11, you need one of two possible throws: 5 and 6, or 6 and 5.

Therefore, the probability is $\frac{2}{36}$. You can grid in the number just like this, without rounding.

5.   The correct answer is that $a = 0$. First, find the slope using the difference of two points, as follows:

$$slope = \frac{8 - 4}{3 - 1} = \frac{4}{2} = 2$$

With a slope of 2, you can now solve for the value of a:

$$2 = \frac{4 - a}{1 - (1)} = \frac{4 - a}{2}$$

$$2 = \frac{4 - 2}{2}$$

$$4 = 4 - a$$

$$0 = a$$

6. The correct answer is 7.13. Isolate the variable and solve for x:

$$10x + 4 = 34 - 6x + 84$$

$$16x + 4 = 34 + 84$$

$$16x = 114$$

$$x = \frac{114}{16} \text{, or } 7.125$$

Rounded to the nearest hundredth, this value is 7.13

7. The correct answer is 6. Simplify the expression by substituting the value of $x = 1$:

$$\sqrt{8x + 8} + \sqrt{2x + 2}$$
$$\sqrt{8(1) + 8} + \sqrt{2(1) + 2}$$
$$= \sqrt{16} + \sqrt{4}$$
$$= 4 + 2 = 6$$

8. The correct answer is 1. This question involves simultaneous questions. Use the method of substitution in order to isolate the variable y:

$$2x + 3y = 11$$

$$-x + 5y = 1 \text{ (multiply by 2)}$$

$$2x + 3y = 11$$

$$-2x + 10y = 2$$

$$13y = 13$$

$$y = 1$$

9. The correct answer is 0. To solve this equation, start by factoring the equation:

$$5x(4x - 3) = 0$$

Now set each product = 0:

$$5x = 0 \quad 4x - 3 = 0$$

$$x = 0 \quad x = \frac{3}{4}$$

The product of these two values, 0 and $\frac{3}{4}$, is 0.

10. The correct answer is 2.4. To solve this proportion, cross multiply:

$$5(3x - 5) = 4(5 - x)$$

$$15x - 25 = 20 - 4x$$

$$19x = 45$$

$$x = \frac{45}{19} \text{, or } 2.368$$

Rounded off, this number equals 2.4

Written Response Explanation

The first thing to do in this problem is to clearly identify and list all of the inequalities that are given in the problem. To ensure that you will receive all possible points, clearly identify each variable you assign:

Let x = number of teachers to be hired

Let y = number of teacher aides to be hired

1. There are three equations given in the problem:

$$x + y \geq 20$$

$$x \geq 12$$

$$2x \geq y$$

2. Next, graph the three equations. A possible graph looks like:

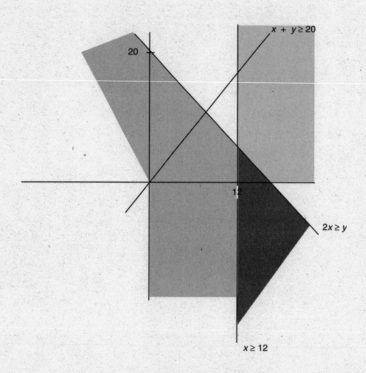

Make sure that each line is a solid line (they are all *greater than* or *equal to*). Also, shade the region to the right that shows the possible set of values.

3. Finally, is it possible to have 10 teachers and 22 teacher aides? No. To determine this answer, test the value of $x = 10$ and $y = 22$ in each equation. If you do so, you will see that these numbers violate the equation $2x \geq y$. Further, you can plot this point on your graph and show that it is not part of the shaded region.

THE PRINCETON REVIEW ALGEBRA GSE PRACTICE TEST III

SESSION ONE

Directions

Make sure you have two or three No. 2 pencils with erasers and a ruler or straightedge available to you during the exam. You also may have a calculator; it may be either a scientific or graphing calculator. You may not use minicomputers, pocket organizers, or calculators with QWERTY (typewriter) keyboards. You may not share your calculator with other students.

Do not spend too much time on a question that seems too difficult. Answer the easier questions first and then return to the harder ones if you have the time. Try to answer every question, even if you have to guess.

Notes:

(1) Figures that accompany problems are drawn as accurately as possible EXCEPT when it is stated that a figure is not drawn to scale. All figures lie in a plane unless otherwise indicated.

(2) All numbers used are real numbers. All algebraic expressions represent real numbers unless otherwise indicated.

1. Ben has a punch that is 80% grape juice, and one that is 30% grape juice. How many liters of the 80% solution are needed to make a 200L solution that is 62% grape juice?

   A. 62

   B 72

   C. 124

   D. 128

2. Which of the following equations represents a line that passes through (4, 7) and (2, 7)?

   A. $4x + 7y = 57$

   B. $4x = 7y - 2$

   C. $x = 7$

   D. $y = 7$

3. The solution set to $|x + 3| = 5$ is:

   A. -2 only

   B. 2 only

   C. -8 only

   D. 2 and -8

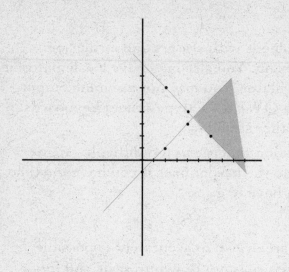

4. The graph above represents which system of inequalities?

 A. $2x + y \geq 8$

   $2x - y > 1$

 B. $2x + y > 8$

   $2x - y \geq 1$

 C. $2x + y > 1$

   $2x - y > 8$

 D. $2x + y \geq 8$

   $2x - y \geq 1$

5. If $.3r - 2.8 = 3.2 - .2r$, then $r =$

 A. .12

 B. $\dfrac{16}{5}$

 C. 6

 D. 12

6. Which of the following lines is NOT perpendicular to $3x + 2y = 16$?

 A. $y = \dfrac{2}{3}x + 7$

 B. $-6y = -4x + 2$

 C. $-6x = -9y + 2$

 D. $2x + 3y = 8$

7. What is the solution to $(x^2 + 3x - 6) + (x^3 + 2x^2 - 4)$?

 A. $x^3 + 3x^2 - x - 6$

 B. $x^3 + 3x^2 + 3x - 2$

 C. $x^3 + 3x^2 + 3x - 10$

 D. $4x^5 - 7x$

8. A rectangle has points $(4, -1)$, $(-3, -1)$, $(4, 6)$ and $(k, 6)$. What is the value of k?

 A. -3

 B. -1

 C. 4

 D. 6

9. What is the value of y if $\sqrt{y + 20} = 4$?

 A. -18

 B. -4

 C. 4

 D. 16

10. If $3b + 2a = 2$ and $-2b + a = 8$, what is the value of a?

 A. -2

 B. 2

 C. 4

 D. 8

11. If $y = 2$, then $(5y)^3 - 75 =$

    A. -45

    B. -35

    C. 25

    D. 925

12. Rewrite 3,600,000 using scientific notation.

    A. 3.6×10^7

    B. 36×10^6

    C. 3.6×10^6

    D. 10×3.6^6

13. A square has a side length of $3a$. What is the perimeter of the square?

    A. $6a$

    B. $12a$

    C. $9a^2$

    D. $12a^4$

14. The area of a square is $\frac{1}{4}a^2$. What is the length of a side of this square?

    A. $2a$

    B. $2a^4$

    C. $\frac{1}{2}a$

    D. $\frac{1}{8}a$

15. A block is chosen at random from a bag that contains 6 white blocks, 4 black blocks, and 12 red blocks. What is the probability that the block will be either a red block or a white block?

    A. $\dfrac{2}{11}$

    B. $\dfrac{3}{11}$

    C. $\dfrac{8}{11}$

    D. $\dfrac{9}{11}$

16. A line with a slope of k passes through points $(4, -1)$ and $(-2, -5)$. What is the value of k?

    A. $-\dfrac{3}{2}$

    B. $-\dfrac{2}{3}$

    C. $\dfrac{2}{3}$

    D. $\dfrac{3}{2}$

17. Which of the following (x, y) coordinates is a solution of the system:

    $$\{y = x + 1\}$$
    $$\{2x + y = 4\}$$

    A. $(2, 3)$

    B. $(0, 4)$

    C. $(-2, -3)$

    D. $(1, 2)$

18. The number of real-number solutions to the equation $x^2 - x + 2 = 0$ is:

    A. 0

    B. 1

    C. 2

    D. Infinitely many

19. Evaluate the expression $(x - 4)^3$ for the value $x = 6$:

    A. 6

    B. 8

    C. 12

    D. 1000

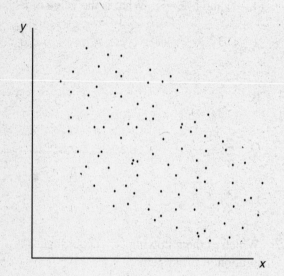

20. Looking at the scatter plot above, what type of relationship exists between the variables in each graph?

    A. A positive relationship

    B. A negative relationship

    C. No relationship

    D. A circular relationship

21. In order to convert between Fahrenheit (°F) and Celsius (°C), you can use the following formula: $°C = \dfrac{5}{9}(°F - 32)$. What is the temperature in Celsius if the Fahrenheit temperature is 68 degrees?

    A. 20

    B. 55.5

    C. 68

    D. 154

22. The value in cents of $(4x + 3)$ quarters is:

    A. $4x + 3$

    B. $16x + 12$

    C. $20x + 15$

    D. $100x + 75$

23. A square has angles represented by the value $27x + 9$. What is the value of x?

    A. 13

    B. 9

    C. 6

    D. 3

24. Chris can complete the puzzle in 10 minutes. Fiona can complete the puzzle in 20 minutes. How long would it take them, working together, to complete the puzzle?

    A. 30 minutes

    B. 20 minutes

    C. $8\dfrac{1}{2}$ minutes

    D. $6\dfrac{2}{3}$ minutes

25. What is the perimeter of a triangle with vertices $(-4, 0)$, $(2, 0)$, and $(-4, 8)$?

   A. 14

   B. 24

   C. 36

   D. 62

26. $10y - 36 + 4y - 6 + y = 3$. What is y?

   A. 3

   B. 4

   C. 6

   D. 10

27. In Allison's class, there are 23 more boys than girls. If there are a total of 81 students in the class, how many girls are in the class?

   A. 23

   B. 29

   C. 40

   D. 52

28. If $(x - 3)$ is a factor of $x^2 - 6x + p$, what is the value of p?

   A. -18

   B. -9

   C. 9

   D. 18

29. On a table are 20 coins, some quarters and some dimes. The total value of the money on the table is $3.05. How many quarters are on the table?

   A. 3

   B. 7

   C. 13

   D. 20

30. Solve for y: $3y - 6 - 7y = 12 - 2y + 6$

   A. -3

   B. 3

   C. 12

   D. -12

1

YOUR NAME: _____
(Print)   Last   First   M.I.

SIGNATURE: _____   DATE: ____ / ____ / ____

HOME ADDRESS: _____
(Print)   Number and Street

_____
City   State   Zip Code

PHONE NO.: _____
(Print)

Completely darken bubbles with a No. 2 pencil. If you make a mistake, be sure to erase mark completely. Erase all stray marks.

Practice Test III

1. Ⓐ Ⓑ Ⓒ Ⓓ   16. Ⓐ Ⓑ Ⓒ Ⓓ
2. Ⓐ Ⓑ Ⓒ Ⓓ   17. Ⓐ Ⓑ Ⓒ Ⓓ
3. Ⓐ Ⓑ Ⓒ Ⓓ   18. Ⓐ Ⓑ Ⓒ Ⓓ
4. Ⓐ Ⓑ Ⓒ Ⓓ   19. Ⓐ Ⓑ Ⓒ Ⓓ
5. Ⓐ Ⓑ Ⓒ Ⓓ   20. Ⓐ Ⓑ Ⓒ Ⓓ
6. Ⓐ Ⓑ Ⓒ Ⓓ   21. Ⓐ Ⓑ Ⓒ Ⓓ
7. Ⓐ Ⓑ Ⓒ Ⓓ   22. Ⓐ Ⓑ Ⓒ Ⓓ
8. Ⓐ Ⓑ Ⓒ Ⓓ   23. Ⓐ Ⓑ Ⓒ Ⓓ
9. Ⓐ Ⓑ Ⓒ Ⓓ   24. Ⓐ Ⓑ Ⓒ Ⓓ
10. Ⓐ Ⓑ Ⓒ Ⓓ   25. Ⓐ Ⓑ Ⓒ Ⓓ
11. Ⓐ Ⓑ Ⓒ Ⓓ   26. Ⓐ Ⓑ Ⓒ Ⓓ
12. Ⓐ Ⓑ Ⓒ Ⓓ   27. Ⓐ Ⓑ Ⓒ Ⓓ
13. Ⓐ Ⓑ Ⓒ Ⓓ   28. Ⓐ Ⓑ Ⓒ Ⓓ
14. Ⓐ Ⓑ Ⓒ Ⓓ   29. Ⓐ Ⓑ Ⓒ Ⓓ
15. Ⓐ Ⓑ Ⓒ Ⓓ   30. Ⓐ Ⓑ Ⓒ Ⓓ

SESSION TWO

Directions

The following questions are similar to the multiple-choice questions, but answer choices are not provided. You must determine the answers yourself using separate scratch paper, and then use a special area on the answer sheet like the one on page 229 to bubble in your answers. If the answer is a mixed numeral, it is to be gridded as a decimal or improper fraction (e.g., $3\frac{1}{2}$ should be gridded as 7/2 or 3.5).

Grid-In Questions

1. A two-sided coin is tossed three times. What is the probability that "heads" will be the result exactly two times?

2. Oil is poured into a large, empty tank at the rate of 500 gallons per minute. At the same time, oil is leaking out at a rate of 300 gallons per minute. If the tank is full in 30 minutes, how many gallons of oil can it hold?

3. If $x + y = 3$ and $x - y = 1$, then $x =$

4. If $a = 4$, $b = -2$, and $c = \frac{1}{2}$, then $2a + (2b)(ab) - 2c - 6abc =$

5. Given the equation $2x = y + 1$, the slope minus the y-intercept equals:

6. If triangle RST has angles that measure $(x + 8)$, $(3x - 12)$, and $(4x + 8)$, then the value of the smallest angle is:

7. Grid in one possible positive value for x if $(x - 6)(x + 6) = 13$:

8. Mel owes money to Elizabeth, Rob, and Ken. Mel owes Elizabeth half the amount he owes Rob and he owes Ken three times the amount he owes Elizabeth. If Mel owes the three a total of $18, then how much does he owe Elizabeth?

9. Judy is 26 years old and Diane is 5 years old. In how many years will Judy be twice as old as Diane?

10. A line perpendicular to $-3x - 6y = 4$ will have a slope of:

Written Response Question

A student was being taught the sport of archery in her physical education class. In the class, she learned how to hold a bow. As she drew the arrow back, the instructor let her know that the further she drew the arrow back, the farther it would travel. To test this, another student recorded the distance of each arrow she shot. Here is what the student recorded:

Distance the Arrow was Drawn Back	Distance the Arrow Traveled
2 in	10 in
3 in	30 in
4 in	68 in
5 in	130 in
6 in	222 in

1. Make a graph of the information above.

2. Predict how far an arrow will travel if the student draws the arrow back 7 inches.

3. Explain how you made this prediction and show your work.

4. Develop a rule that describes the relationship between the amount an arrow is drawn back and the length the arrow will travel.

GRID-IN ANSWER SHEET

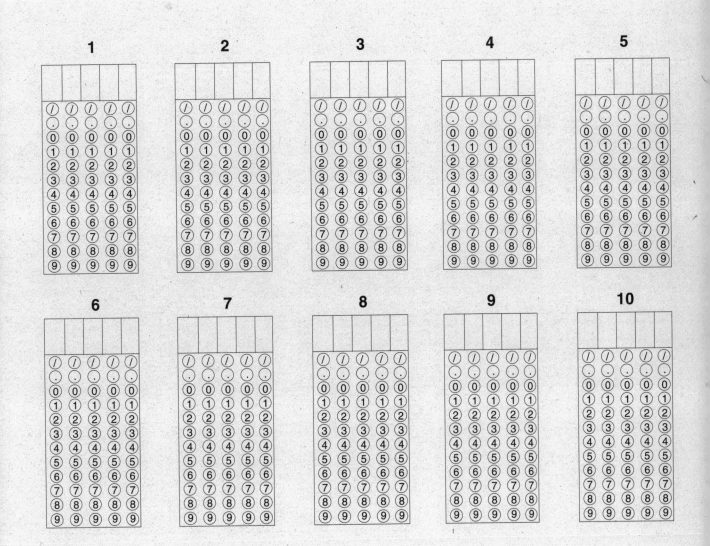

WRITTEN RESPONSE
ANSWER SHEET

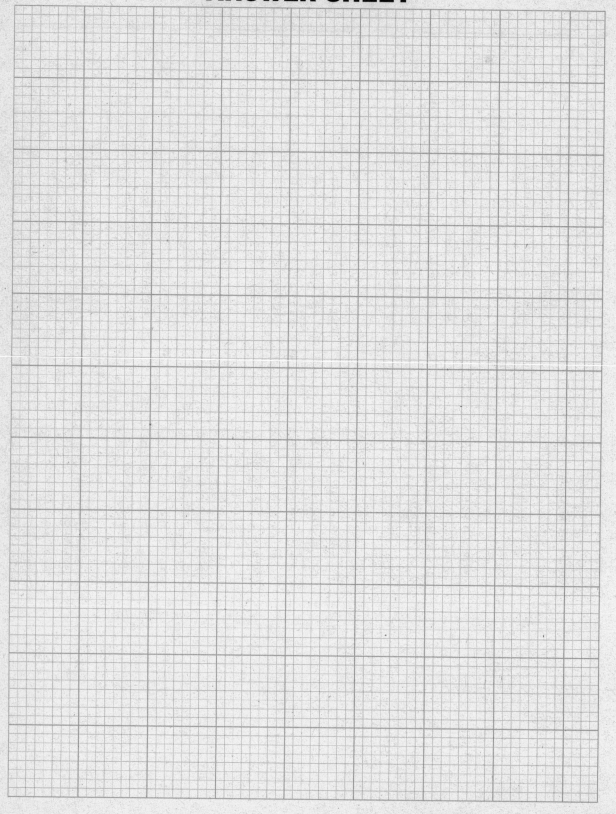

ANSWERS AND EXPLANATIONS FOR SESSION ONE

Answer Key

1.	D	11.	D	21.	A
2.	D	12.	C	22.	D
3.	D	13.	B	23.	D
4.	A	14.	C	24.	D
5.	D	15.	D	25.	B
6.	D	16.	C	26.	A
7.	C	17.	D	27.	B
8.	A	18.	A	28.	C
9.	B	19.	B	29.	B
10.	C	20.	B	30.	D

Explanations

1. Ben has a punch that is 80% grape juice, and one that is 30% grape juice. How many liters of the 80% solution must be combined with the 30% grape juice to make a 200L solution that is 62% grape juice?

    A. 62

    B   72

    C. 124

    D. 128

1. The correct answer is D. In order to solve this mixture problem set up a chart like the one below:

	Percent Grape Juice	Amount of Solution	Amount of Mixture
First Solution	80%	x	$.8x$
Second Solution	30%	$200-x$	$60-.3x$
Third Solution	62%	200	$(.62)(200)$

Therefore, you can set up an equation to give you the following:

$$.8x + (60 - .3x) = (.62)(200)$$

$$.8x + 60 - .3x = 124$$

$$.5x = 64$$

$$x = 128$$

You can also Ballpark to eliminate C and D, and guess, if you're desperate!

2. Which of the following equations represents a line that passes through (4, 7) and (2, 7)?

A. $4x + 7y = 57$

B. $4x = 7y - 2$

C. $x = 7$

D. $y = 7$

2. Answer choice D is correct. When you are given two points in a line, you can use them to determine the slope, y-intercept, etc. But on this test, it is usually easier to simply plug in the sets of numbers to see in which answer choices work. Here the slope is 0. This tells us the equation should have no x value, and $y = 7$ is the correct equation.

3. The solution set to $|x + 3| = 5$ is:

A. -2 only

B. 2 only

C. -8 only

D. 2 and -8

3. The correct answer is D. You should also simply Backsolve this question by plugging in the answer choices. 2 works. $|5| = 5$. -8 also works; $|-5| = 5$, and D is correct. If you wanted to set up a series of equations, you would set up the following:

$$x + 3 = 5 \text{ or } x + 3 = -5$$

Solve for each question independently to get the answer.

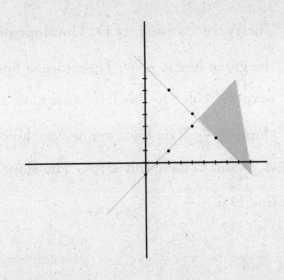

4. The graph above represents which system of inequalities?

   A. $2x + y \geq 8$

       $2x - y > 1$

   B. $2x + y > 8$

       $2x - y \geq 1$

   C. $2x + y > 1$

       $2x - y > 8$

   D. $2x + y \geq 8$

       $2x - y \geq 1$

4. The correct answer is A. The $2x + y$ is a straight line, so eliminate B and C. The $2x - y$ line is a dotted line, so eliminate D.

5. If $.3r - 2.8 = 3.2 - .2r$, then $r =$

   A. .12

   B. $\dfrac{16}{5}$

   C. 6

   D. 12

5. The correct answer is D. First rearrange the equation to isolate the variable: $.5r = 6.0$; now, divide by .5 to solve for r, and $r = 12$.

6. Which of the following lines is NOT perpendicular to $3x + 2y = 16$?

   A. $y = \dfrac{2}{3}x + 7$

   B. $-6y = -4x + 2$

   C. $-6x = -9y + 2$

   D. $2x + 3y = 8$

6. The correct answer is D. The slope of the given line is $-\dfrac{3}{2}$. Therefore, a line perpendicular to this line must have a slope of $\dfrac{2}{3}$. The lines in answer choices A, B and C have this slope. The slope of line D is $-\dfrac{2}{3}$.

7. What is the solution to $(x^2 + 3x - 6) + (x^3 + 2x^2 - 4)$?

   A. $x^3 + 3x^2 - x - 6$

   B. $x^3 + 3x^2 + 3x - 2$

   C. $x^3 + 3x^2 + 3x - 10$

   D. $4x^5 - 7x$

7. Answer choice C is correct. Remember that when you're adding, you can only combine like variables (same letter, and to the same power).

8. A rectangle has points $(4, -1)$, $(-3, -1)$, $(4, 6)$ and $(k, 6)$. What is the value of k?

   A. -3

   B. -1

   C. 4

   D. 6

8. The correct answer is A. Go ahead and graph the first three points to find where the missing point of the rectangle should be. In order for the four points to form a rectangle, which contains only right angles, the missing point is at $(-3, 6)$, and, k must be -3.

9. What is the value of y if $\sqrt{y + 20} = 4$?

   A. -18

   B. -4

   C. 4

   D. 16

9. The correct answer is B. To find y, square both sides of each equation to get: $y + 20 = 16$. Move the y to the right hand side to get $y = -4$.

10. If $3b + 2a = 2$ and $-2b + a = 8$, what is the value of a?

    A. -2

    B. 2

    C. 4

    D. 8

10. The correct answer is C. To find the value of a, use the substitution method, shown below. Note that we chose to multiply the equations to eliminate the variable. This will save you extra time. By solving for a instead of b, you won't have to go back to the equations.

$3b + 2a = 2$ (multiply by 2) $6b + 4a = 4$

$-2b + a = 8$ (multiply by 3) $\underline{-6b + 3a = 24}$

$$7a = 28$$

$$a = 4$$

You could also use the substitution method:

$$3b + 2(8 + 2b) = 2$$

$$3b + 16 + 4b = 2$$

$$b = -2$$

$$-2(2) + a = 8$$

$$a = 4$$

11. If $y = 2$, then $(5y)^3 - 75 =$

    A. -45

    B. -35

    C. 25

    D. 925

11. The correct answer is D. First you need to substitute the value of 2 in for y in the equation, and using the order of operations,

$$(5 \times 2)^3 - 75 =$$

$$(10)^3 - 75 =$$

$$1000 - 75 = 925$$

12. Rewrite 3,600,000 using scientific notation:

   A. 3.6×10^7

   B. 36×10^6

   C. 3.6×10^6

   D. 10×3.6^6

12. The correct answer is C. To rewrite the number, count the number of places you need to move the decimal to the right of the units place. In the problem, it takes 6 places to move to the right of the 3. If we rewrite the number as 3.6, we need to add 6 places to the right. This is done by multiplying by 10^6, and the correct answer is C.

13. A square has a length of side 3a. What is the perimeter of the square?

   A. $6a$

   B. $12a$

   C. $9a^2$

   D. $12a^4$

13. The correct answer is B. A square has four equal sides. To find the perimeter, we add: $3a + 3a + 3a + 3a$, or $4 \times 3a$. $12a$ is the correct answer.

14. The area of a square is $\frac{1}{4}a^2$. What is the length of a side of this square?

   A. $2a$

   B. $2a^4$

   C. $\frac{1}{2}a$

   D. $\frac{1}{8}a$

14. The correct answer is C. The area of a square is the value of one of its sides, squared. Thus, to get the value of $\frac{1}{4}a^2$, we needed to square a term. Take the square root of the area to get $\frac{1}{2}a^2$, and that's your answer.

15. A block is chosen at random from a bag that contains 6 white blocks, 4 black blocks, and 12 red blocks. What is the probability that the block will be either a red block or a white block?

   A. $\dfrac{2}{11}$

   B. $\dfrac{3}{11}$

   C. $\dfrac{8}{11}$

   D. $\dfrac{9}{11}$

15. Answer choice D is correct. There are a total of 22 blocks. The outcome we are looking for (red or white) constitutes 18 possibilities, so the probability is $\dfrac{18}{22}$, or $\dfrac{9}{11}$.

16. A line with a slope of k passes through points $(4, -1)$ and $(-2, -5)$. What is the value of k?

   A. $-\dfrac{3}{2}$

   B. $-\dfrac{2}{3}$

   C. $\dfrac{2}{3}$

   D. $\dfrac{3}{2}$

16. The correct answer is C. Don't worry about the extra variable here—just find the slope of the line. The slope can be found by putting the difference of the y's over the difference of the x's:

$$\frac{[-5-(-1)]}{[-2-4]}=\frac{-4}{-6}=\frac{2}{3}$$

17. Which of the following (x, y) coordinates is a solution of the system:

$$\{y = x + 1\}$$

$$\{2x + y = 4\}$$

A. (2, 3)

B. (0, 4)

C. (–2, –3)

D. (1, 2)

17. Answer choice D is correct. Normally, when given a system of two equations, you would need to use the substitution method to find the values of x and y. But here, with answer choices available to you, simply plug them in to see which one works. Only answer choice D will give you the correct answer. Note: If you did want to substitute, you should use the value of y from the first equation and plug into the second:

$$2x + (x + 1) = 4$$

$$3x + 1 = 4$$

$$3x = 3$$

$$x = 1$$

Substitute back into any equation to get y:

$$y = (1) + 1$$

$$y = 2$$

18. The number of real-number solutions to the equation $x^2 - x + 2 = 0$ is:

A. 0

B. 1

C. 2

D. Infinitely many

18. The correct answer is A. In order to find the number of real-number solutions that exist for an equation, you need to evaluate part of the quadratic formula, known as the discriminant. The discriminant is defined as the number that's underneath the square root sign in the quadratic formula, $b^2 - 4ac$. From the equation above, we know that $a = 1$, $b = -1$, and $c = 2$, so:

$$b^2 - 4ac = (-1)^2 - 4(1)(2) =$$

$$1 - 8 = -7$$

A negative value for the discriminant means that there are no real-number solutions.

19. Evaluate the expression $(x - 4)^3$ for the value $x = 6$:

   A. 6

   B. 8

   C. 12

   D. 1000

19. The answer is B. Substitute the value 6 in for x in the equation. Doing so leaves us with the equation:

$$(6 - 4)^3$$

This simplifies to 2 raised to the third power:

$$2 \times 2 \times 2 = 8.$$

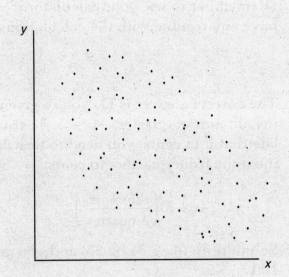

20. Looking at the scatter plot above, what type of relationship exists between the variables in each graph?

   A. A positive relationship

   B. A negative relationship

   C. No relationship

   D. A circular relationship

20. The answer is B. In order to determine a relationship represented by a scattergram, remember to draw the line of best fit. Here, the line of best fit indicates a negative relationship between the two variables because it has a negative slope.

21. In order to convert between Fahrenheit (°F) and Celsius (°C), you can use the following formula: $C = \dfrac{5}{9}(F - 32)$. What is the temperature in Celsius if the Fahrenheit temperature is 68 degrees?

A. 20

B. 55.5

C. 68

D. 154

21. Answer choice A is the correct answer. In order to solve this equation, you need to substitute the value 68 into the equation for F:

$$C = \frac{5}{9}(68 - 32)$$

$$C = \frac{5}{9}(36)$$

$$C = 20$$

(Remember to use your calculator if you have any trouble with the calculations!)

22. The value in cents of $(4x + 3)$ quarters is:

A. $4x + 3$

B. $16x + 12$

C. $20x + 15$

D. $100x + 75$

22. The correct answer is D. You're given the amount of quarters, $4x + 3$. To translate that into cents, you need to translate the units from quarters to cents:

$$(4x + 3)\left(\frac{25 \text{ cents}}{1 \text{ quarter}}\right)$$

So multiply $(4x + 3)$ by 25, and you get $100x + 75$.

23. A square has angles represented by the value $27x + 9$. What is the value of x?

A. 13

B. 9

C. 6

D. 3

23. The correct answer is D. Every angle in a square is equal to 90 degrees. To find the value of x, set the equation $27x + 9 = 90$; so $27x = 81$, and $x = 3$.

24. Chris can complete the puzzle in 10 minutes. Fiona can complete the puzzle in 20 minutes. How long would it take them, working together, to complete the puzzle?

A. 30 minutes

B. 20 minutes

C. $8\frac{1}{2}$ minutes

D. $6\frac{2}{3}$ minutes

24. The correct answer is D. Use POE to eliminate answer choices A and B because they don't make sense. Then translate the work rates of Chris and Fiona into a common unit:

Chris can do $\frac{1}{10}$ of the job per minute

Fiona can do $\frac{1}{20}$ of the job per minute

Together, $\frac{1}{10} + \frac{1}{20}$ is their rate per minute. $\frac{1}{10} + \frac{1}{20} = \frac{3}{20}$. This is their rate, and to finish the puzzle,

$$\frac{3}{20}t = 1$$
$$\text{and } t = \frac{20}{3}$$

So it takes them $\frac{20}{3}$ minutes to finish the job.

25. What is the perimeter of a triangle with vertices (–4, 0), (2, 0), and (–4, 8)?

A. 14

B. 24

C. 36

D. 62

25. The correct answer is B. First, use the points to draw out the triangle you are given. You will find that the triangle looks something like this:

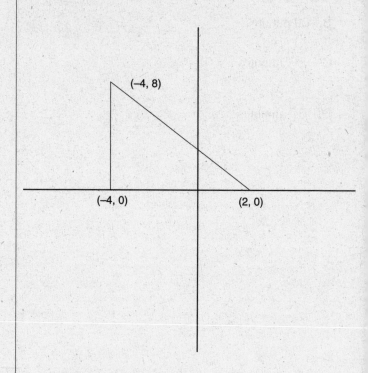

The base of the triangle is 6. The height of the triangle is 8. To find the length of the third side, think of the Pythagorean triplets. This is a 6-8-10 triangle, so the perimeter is 6 + 8 + 10 = 24. But if you hadn't memorized the triplets, you could still use the Pythagorean theorem, $a^2 + b^2 = c^2$, where c is the hypotenuse.

$$(6)^2 + (8)^2 = c^2$$

$$36 + 64 = c^2$$

$$100 = c^2$$

$$c = 10$$

and 6 + 8 + 10 = 24

26. $10y - 36 + 4y - 6 + y = 3$. What is y?

    A. 3

    B. 4

    C. 6

    D. 10

26. Answer choice A is correct. Simplify to get:

$$15y - 42 = 3$$

$$15y = 45$$

$$y = 3$$

27. In Allison's class, there are 23 more boys than girls. If there are a total of 81 students in the class, how many girls are in the class?

    A. 23

    B. 29

    C. 40

    D. 52

27. Answer Choice B is correct. This question is best solved by Backsolving. First, you can eliminate answer choices C and D; if there are more boys in the class, then the class will have less than 50% girls, and these two answer choices are too high. To Backsolve, start with one of the remaining answer choices. If you select B, you're saying that there are 29 girls in the class. This would mean that there are 23 more boys, for a total of 52 boys. 29 girls and 52 boys give us the desired total of 81 students in the class.

28. If $(x - 3)$ is a factor of $x^2 - 6x + p$, what is the value of p?

    A −18

    B. −9

    C. 9

    D. 18

28. The correct answer is C. In order to find the value of p, you need to use the information to properly factor the polynomial. Look at the middle term, $-6x$. You know that this term is created by adding two coefficients together. Because you have -3, we know that the next factored term will include -3 (because $-3 + -3 = -6$). After factoring, you'll find that the equation is now $(x - 3)(x - 3)$. When you expand this, the value of $p = 9$.

29. On a table are 20 coins, some quarters and some dimes. The total value of the money on the table is $3.05. How many quarters are on the table?

    A. 3

    B. 7

    C. 13

    D. 20

29. The correct answer is B. There are two ways to approach this challenging question. One is to write out simultaneous questions. The second is to Backsolve! Let the answer choices do the work for you. Start by seeing if you can eliminate any answer choice by Ballparking. D is incorrect because there can't only be quarters on the table (the total value would be too high). Cross that out and move to answer choice C. If there were 13 quarters, the value of the quarters would be 13 × $.25 = $3.25. This, too, is already over the total of $3.05, so eliminate C. Now try B: 7 quarters gives us a total value of 7 × $.25 = $1.75. There would be 13 dimes left over, and at $.10 a piece, the total value of dimes is $1.30. Their sum is $3.05; the answer we are looking for.

30. Solve for y: $3y - 6 - 7y = 12 - 2y + 6$

    A. −3

    B. 3

    C. 12

    D. −12

30. D is the correct answer. To solve this question, make sure you get all terms that contain variables on the same side of the equation:

$$-4y - 6 = 18 - 2y$$

$$-2y = 24$$

$$y = -12$$

ANSWERS AND EXPLANATIONS FOR SESSION TWO

Grid-In Answer Key

1. $\frac{3}{8}$ or .375

2. 6,000 gallons

3. 2

4. 63

5. 3

6. 30

7. 7

8. 3

9. 16

10. 2

Grid-In Explanations

1. The correct answer is $\frac{3}{8}$, or .375 if you grid in with a decimal. To find this combined probability, it is probably easiest to write out the possibilities.

    There are two outcomes with each toss of the coin. If it is done three times, there are $2 \times 2 \times 2$ outcomes, or 8 total outcomes. They can be labeled as follows:

H	H	H		**H**	**H**	**T**
H	**T**	**H**		H	T	T
T	T	T		T	T	H
T	H	T		**T**	**H**	**H**

    Of these outcomes, you can see that three of them have exactly heads twice. The probability is $\frac{3}{8}$.

2. The correct answer is 6,000 gallons. This is a question that deals with rates. There are a total of 200 gallons being added per minute to the tank (500 gallons – 300 gallons that leak out). If this runs for 30 minutes, we have:

$$\frac{200 \text{ gallons}}{\text{minute}}(30 \text{ minutes}) = 6000 \text{ gallons}$$

3. The correct answer is 2. To find the value of x with this system of equations, add the two equations together:

$$x + y = 3$$
$$x - y = 1$$
$$2x = 4$$
$$x = 2$$

4. The correct answer is 63. To find the correct answer, simply substitute the values for the variables, and then use the rules of PEMDAS to solve the problem:

$$2a + (2b)(ab) - 2c - 6abc =$$

$$2(4) + (2)(-2)(4)(-2) - 2\left(\frac{1}{2}\right) - 6(4)(-2)\left(\frac{1}{2}\right) =$$

$$8 + (-4)(-8) - 1 - (-24) =$$

$$8 + 32 - 1 + 24 =$$

$$40 - 1 + 24 =$$

$$39 + 24 = 63$$

5. The correct answer is 3. To find the correct answer, first put the equation in the proper $y = mx + b$ format:

$$2x = y + 1$$
$$y = 2x - 1$$

The slope is 2, and the y-intercept is -1. Therefore the slope minus the y-intercept is

$$(2) - (-1) = 3$$

6. The correct answer is 30. You know that the sum of the angles in a triangle is 180, so set up an equation to find the value of x:

$$(x + 8) + (3x - 12) + (4x + 8) = 180$$

$$8x + 4 = 180$$

$$8x = 176$$

$$x = 22$$

Therefore, the angles are 30, 54, and 96. Be sure to grid in the value 30, and not the value of x (22)!

7. The correct answer is 7. Expand this equation to get it in standard form:

$$(x - 6)(x + 6) = 13$$

$$x^2 - 36 = 13$$

$$x^2 = 49$$

$$x^2 - 49 = 0$$

$$(x + 7)(x - 7) = 0$$

$$x = -7, 7$$

Now grid in the positive value, 7.

8. The correct answer is 3. We can summarize the amount of money Mel owes with the following equation:

$$\$18 = E + R + K$$

We know something about the relationship between the amount of money those three are owed. Specifically,

$$2E = R \quad \text{(from the first statement)}$$

$$3E = K \quad \text{(from the second statement)}$$

With this information, we can substitute to find that

$$\$18 = E + 2E + 3E$$

$$\$18 = 6E$$

$$3 = E$$

9. The correct answer is 16. We want to get to a point where Judy's age (J), is twice that of Diane's (D). We can set up this equation to show what we are looking for:

$$(J + x) = 2(D + x)$$

where x is the number of years.

$$26 + x = 10 + 2x$$

$$16 = x$$

10. The correct answer is 2. First find the slope of the line in the problem:

$$-3x - 6y = 4$$

$$-6y = 3x - 4$$

$$6y = -3x + 4$$

$$y = -\frac{1}{2} + \frac{2}{3}$$

If the slope of this line is $-\frac{1}{2}$, the slope of a line perpendicular to it must have a slope of 2. Remember that perpendicular lines have reciprocal slopes.

Written Response Explanation

To receive the highest possible score (4), be sure that you have clearly shown your work on all parts of the question. First you need to graph the information. Your graph should look something like this:

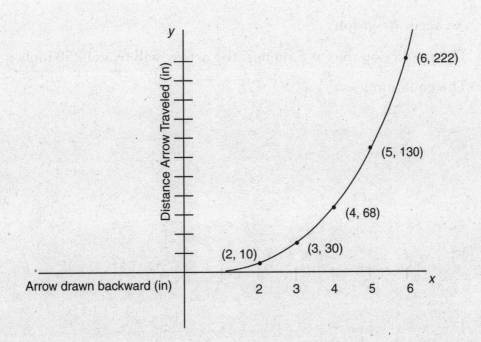

As you can see above, a complete graph includes labeled x and y coordinates; representation of the points, and is easy to read and clear.

Now try to predict the relationship between the two variables, by looking for a pattern. 3 yields 30, so at first glance, you might assume that the number gets multiplied by ten. But this is not true if you look at the second set of numbers— 4 yields 68. If you find that a simple factor will not determine an equation, try to work with exponents. In this case, if you label the distance an arrow is drawn backward x, and the amount the arrow will travel, y, one accurate equation is:

$$y = x^3 + x$$

Try this equation out on a couple of numbers to be sure it works. This equation will then allow you to calculate the projected distance of an arrow if you draw the arrow 7 inches back from the bow. Putting $x = 7$ into the equation:

$$y = 7^3 + 7$$

$$y = 243 + 7$$

$$y = 250 \text{ inches}$$

When solving the distance traveled, be sure to label the distance, and be sure to cite the equation you used to solve for y, *even if the equation is written elsewhere in your response.* Always err on the side of *repeating* information, or restating information that you found from previous calculations.

A complete score requires:

- An accurate graph

- The prediction that at 7 inches, the arrow will travel 250 inches

- The equation $y = x^3 + x$

THE PRINCETON REVIEW
ALGEBRA GSE
PRACTICE TEST IV

SESSION ONE

Directions

Make sure you have two or three No. 2 pencils with erasers and a ruler or straightedge available to you during the exam. You also may have a calculator; it may be either a scientific or graphing calculator. You may not use minicomputers, pocket organizers, or calculators with QWERTY (typewriter) keyboards. You may not share your calculator with other students.

Do not spend too much time on a question that seems too difficult. Answer the easier questions first and then return to the harder ones if you have the time. Try to answer every question, even if you have to guess.

Notes:

(1) Figures that accompany problems are drawn as accurately as possible EXCEPT when it is stated that a figure is not drawn to scale. All figures lie in a plane unless otherwise indicated.

(2) All numbers used are real numbers. All algebraic expressions represent real numbers unless otherwise indicated.

1. A rectangle has angles with the value $3x - 6$. What is the value of x?

   A. 32

   B. 30

   C. 24

   D. 17

2. Karen can complete a report in 30 minutes. At this rate, how many reports can she complete in 4 hours?

   A. 2

   B. 4

   C. 8

   D. 120

3. If $(2x + 1)$ is a factor of $2x^2 + 9x + r$, then what is the value of r?

   A. 4

   B. 11

   C. 18

   D. 22

4. At his office, Adam did a survey on what his employees wanted for lunch; sandwiches or pizza. Adam received 34 more votes for pizza than sandwiches. If Adam received a total of 76 votes, how many votes did he receive for sandwiches?

   A. 21

   B. 40

   C. 42

   D. 84

5. Ben can hammer 5 nails a minute. Alex can hammer 4 nails a minute. If Ben and Alex work together, approximately how many minutes will it take to hammer 100 nails?

   A.   7 minutes

   B.   8 minutes

   C.   11 minutes

   D.   13 minutes

6. What is the perimeter of a triangle with vertices $(2, -1)$, $(6, -1)$, and $(6, -4)$?

   A.   7

   B.   9

   C.   12

   D.   14

7. Clint scored a 94 on his biology test. That was 8 more points than his average on his first four tests. In order to find his combined score on all five tests, which of the following equations can be used to solve the problem?

   A. $4x + 94 = 86$

   B. $86 + 94 \times 4 = x$

   C. $(86 \times 4) + 94 = x$

   D. $(94 \times 4) = x - 86$

8. At a local high school, x out of every 5 students go to Butterick College. If there are 240 students, how many are expected to go to Butterick College?

   A. $12x$ students

   B. $48x$ students

   C. $60x$ students

   D. $235x$ students

9. Right triangle ABC has lengths of 3, 4, and a hypotenuse of x. Right triangle DEF has lengths of x, 12, and a hypotenuse of y. What is the value of $x + y$?

   A.   5

   B.   12

   C.   13

   D.   18

10. Kathleen has two coins. What is the probability that, after flipping those coins, she will get one head and one tail?

   A.   1

   B. $\dfrac{3}{4}$

   C. $\dfrac{1}{2}$

   D. $\dfrac{1}{4}$

11. Find two numbers that have a sum of 58 and a difference of 16:

   A.   5, 21

   B.   16, 42

   C.   21, 37

   D. -16, 74

12. If $x = 5$, find the value of $\dfrac{4x + 2}{2x}$.

   A.   4

   B.   5

   C.   2.2

   D.   220

13. A rectangle has sides $(3a - 7)$ and $(5a + 4)$. What is the perimeter of the rectangle?

   A. $8a - 3$

   B. $15a - 28$

   C. $6a - 14$

   D. $16a - 6$

14. What is the solution to $(x^2 + 2x - 9) + (x - 2)$?

   A. $x^3 + 2x^2 - 11$

   B. $x^2 + 3x - 9x - 11$

   C. $x^2 + 3x - 11$

   D. $x^3 + 2x^2 - 11x$

15. If $\sqrt{2y - 7} = \sqrt{3 + 4y}$, what is the value of y?

   A. -10

   B. -5

   C. 5

   D. 8

16. What is the range of the equation $y = x^2$?

   A. All real numbers

   B. All negative real numbers

   C. All positive real numbers

   D. All real numbers greater than or equal to 0

17. $\dfrac{4.5 \times 10^7}{9.0 \times 10^3} =$

   A. 5×10^{10}

   B. 5×10^3

   C. 5×10^4

   D. 5×10^{10}

18. A line with slope 2 passes through $(-6, 7)$ and $(2, p)$. What is the value of p?

   A. 2

   B. 11

   C. 14

   D. 23

19. The solution set to $|2x - 4| = 10$ is:

   A. -10 only

   B. -3 only

   C. -10 and -3

   D. -3 and 7

20. The solution of $|2y - 6| = -9$ is:

   A. $-\dfrac{2}{3}, \dfrac{3}{2}$

   B. $-\dfrac{3}{2}, \dfrac{15}{2}$

   C. $-\dfrac{2}{3}, \dfrac{7}{2}$

   D. $-\dfrac{2}{3}, -\dfrac{3}{2}$

21. If $9a - 6 = 30 - 3a$, then $a =$

   A. 2

   B. 3

   C. 4

   D. 6

22. Marty keeps a collection of pennies, nickels, and dimes in his desk. If he has twice as many dimes as nickels, three times as many pennies as dimes, and $6x$ worth of pennies, then the value of his pennies, nickels, and dimes in cents equals:

    A. $360x$

    B. $100x$

    C. $31x$

    D. x

23. Solve the following equation for w:
    $.83w + .29 = .5w - .7$

    A. $-.3$

    B. -3

    C. -3.3

    D. 3.3

24. A solution of paint that is 100% yellow is to be combined with a solution that is 80% yellow to make 50L of paint that is 84% yellow. How many liters of the 100% yellow solution are needed?

    A. 42

    B. 40

    C. 10

    D. 8

25. Ana is playing a card game. He is holding 5 diamonds and 3 clubs. If he plays two cards at random, what is the probability that he plays two diamonds?

    A. $\dfrac{5}{14}$

    B. $\dfrac{25}{56}$

    C. $\dfrac{9}{14}$

    D. $\dfrac{67}{56}$

26. Simplify the following expression:

    $$\frac{(4a^2b^5)^3}{(2a^1b^0)^2}$$

    A. $16a^4b^{15}$

    B. $3a^7b^{13}$

    C. $16a^7b^{13}$

    D. $3a^7b^{15}$

27. Which of the following (a, b) coordinates is a solution of the system?

    $$\{a + b = -1\}$$
    $$\{b + 3a = 4\}$$

    A. $\left(\dfrac{7}{2}, \dfrac{5}{2}\right)$

    B. $\left(\dfrac{7}{2}, -\dfrac{5}{2}\right)$

    C. $\left(\dfrac{5}{2}, \dfrac{7}{2}\right)$

    D. $\left(\dfrac{5}{2}, -\dfrac{7}{2}\right)$

28. Which of the following lines is parallel to $3x - y = -5$?

    A. $y = 5x - 3$

    B. $y = 4x - 5$

    C. $5y - 15x = 10$

    D. $15y - 5x = 3$

29. The area of a rectangle is $4a^2 + 14a + 12$. If the length of the rectangle is $(2a + 3)$, what is the value of the width of the rectangle?

    A. $2a + 11$

    B. $a^4 + 8a + 9$

    C. $2a + 3$

    D. $2a + 4$

30. A square has sides $(-3, 0)$, $(1, -3)$, $(4, 1)$ and $(0, k)$. What is the value of k?

    A. 1

    B. 3

    C. 4

    D. 5

1

YOUR NAME: _____
(Print)   Last   First   M.I.

SIGNATURE: _____ DATE: ___/___/___

HOME ADDRESS: _____
(Print)   Number and Street

_____
City   State   Zip Code

PHONE NO.: _____
(Print)

Completely darken bubbles with a No. 2 pencil. If you make a mistake, be sure to erase mark completely. Erase all stray marks.

Practice Test IV

1. Ⓐ Ⓑ Ⓒ Ⓓ
2. Ⓐ Ⓑ Ⓒ Ⓓ
3. Ⓐ Ⓑ Ⓒ Ⓓ
4. Ⓐ Ⓑ Ⓒ Ⓓ
5. Ⓐ Ⓑ Ⓒ Ⓓ
6. Ⓐ Ⓑ Ⓒ Ⓓ
7. Ⓐ Ⓑ Ⓒ Ⓓ
8. Ⓐ Ⓑ Ⓒ Ⓓ
9. Ⓐ Ⓑ Ⓒ Ⓓ
10. Ⓐ Ⓑ Ⓒ Ⓓ
11. Ⓐ Ⓑ Ⓒ Ⓓ
12. Ⓐ Ⓑ Ⓒ Ⓓ
13. Ⓐ Ⓑ Ⓒ Ⓓ
14. Ⓐ Ⓑ Ⓒ Ⓓ
15. Ⓐ Ⓑ Ⓒ Ⓓ

16. Ⓐ Ⓑ Ⓒ Ⓓ
17. Ⓐ Ⓑ Ⓒ Ⓓ
18. Ⓐ Ⓑ Ⓒ Ⓓ
19. Ⓐ Ⓑ Ⓒ Ⓓ
20. Ⓐ Ⓑ Ⓒ Ⓓ
21. Ⓐ Ⓑ Ⓒ Ⓓ
22. Ⓐ Ⓑ Ⓒ Ⓓ
23. Ⓐ Ⓑ Ⓒ Ⓓ
24. Ⓐ Ⓑ Ⓒ Ⓓ
25. Ⓐ Ⓑ Ⓒ Ⓓ
26. Ⓐ Ⓑ Ⓒ Ⓓ
27. Ⓐ Ⓑ Ⓒ Ⓓ
28. Ⓐ Ⓑ Ⓒ Ⓓ
29. Ⓐ Ⓑ Ⓒ Ⓓ
30. Ⓐ Ⓑ Ⓒ Ⓓ

SESSION TWO

Directions

The following questions are similar to the multiple-choice questions, but answer choices are not provided. You must determine the answers yourself using separate scratch paper, and then use a special area on the answer sheet like the one on page 263 to bubble in your answers. If the answer is a mixed numeral, it is to be gridded as a decimal or improper fraction (e.g., $3\frac{1}{2}$ should be gridded as $\frac{7}{2}$ or 3.5).

Grid-In Questions

1. Solve the following equation and give the answer to the nearest tenth:

$$7y - 2 = 22 - 4(-8 - y)$$

2. If $4(2x - 3y) = 2(-6y - 3x) + 28$, then $x =$

3. If the sum of four consecutive integers is 86, what is the least of these integers?

4. If $x^2 - 7 = 28$, what is the value of $x^2 + 7$?

5. If $-1 < x < 3$ and $4 < y < 5$, what is one possible value for $x + y$?

6. If $(y + 4)$ is a factor of $2y^2 + 5y - k$, what is the value of k?

7. Mike is holding a bucket of marbles that contains 7 black marbles and 4 red marbles. If he randomly picks two marbles, what is the probability that he will select two red marbles?

8. One more than a positive number times one less than a positive number is 24. Grid in the number.

9. A line passes through (5, 3), (6, 6), and (y, 12). What is the value of y?

10. If $\frac{7}{y} - \frac{1}{3} = \frac{1}{4}$, then $y =$

Written Response Question

Given the following quadratic equation:

$$2x^2 + 3x - 3 = 0$$

perform the following:

1. Solve for x by completing the square.

2. Identify the number of real-number solutions by using the discriminant.

3. Identify the values of a, b, and c in the quadratic formula.

4. Draw a graph of the equation $y = 2x^2 + 3x - 3$ from the information you find in parts 1–3.

Remember to show all parts of your solution, and explain how you arrive at your answers.

GRID-IN ANSWER SHEET

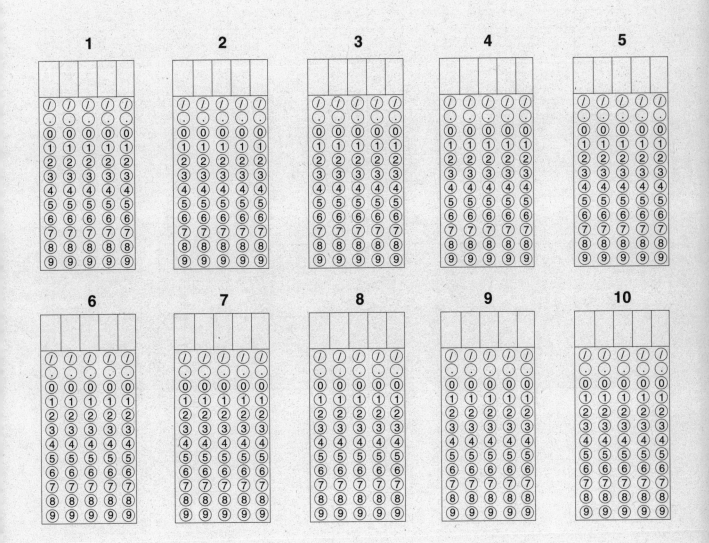

WRITTEN RESPONSE
ANSWER SHEET

ANSWERS AND EXPLANATIONS FOR SESSION ONE

Answer Key

1.	A	11.	C	21.	B
2.	C	12.	C	22.	C
3.	A	13.	D	23.	B
4.	A	14.	C	24.	C
5.	C	15.	B	25.	A
6.	C	16.	D	26.	A
7.	C	17.	B	27.	D
8.	B	18.	D	28.	C
9.	D	19.	D	29.	D
10.	C	20.	B	30.	C

Explanations

1. A rectangle has angles with the value $3x - 6$. What is the value of x?

    A. 32

    B. 30

    C. 24

    D. 17

1. Answer choice A is correct. Remember that all the angles in a rectangle are equal to 90 degrees. Set the value equal to 90 to find the value of x.
    If $3x - 6 = 90$; $3x = 96$, and $x = 32$.

2. Karen can complete a report in 30 minutes. At this rate, how many reports can she complete in 4 hours?

    A. 2

    B. 4

    C. 8

    D. 120

2. The correct answer is C. Karen can do two reports in one hour. Multiply this by 4 to find that she can do 8 reports in 4 hours.

3. If $(2x + 1)$ is a factor of $2x^2 + 9x + r$, then what is the value of r?

A. 4

B. 11

C. 18

D. 22

3. Answer choice A is correct. Using FOIL, you can fill in the information you're given:

$$(2x + 1)(x + ?)$$

If you multiply this out, you get

$$2x^2 + x + ?2x + ?$$

Now, you need to get to $9x$. To do so, you can multiply $2x$ by 4. This, combined with $1x$, will give us a total of $9x$, and r is 4.

4. At his office, Adam did a survey on what his employees wanted for lunch; sandwiches or pizza. Adam received 34 more votes for pizza than sandwiches. If Adam received a total of 76 votes, how many votes did he receive for sandwiches?

A. 21

B. 40

C. 42

D. 84

4. Answer choice A is correct. Ballpark to find the correct answer. First, if there were more pizza votes than sandwich votes, the number of sandwich votes needs to be less than half the total number of votes. Only answer choice A is less than half of the total number of votes. Look at the answer choices before you start to write an algebraic equation.

5. Ben can hammer 5 nails a minute. Alex can hammer 4 nails a minute. If Ben and Alex work together, approximately how many minutes will it take to hammer 100 nails?

A. 7 minutes

B. 8 minutes

C. 11 minutes

D. 13 minutes

5. C is the correct answer. Together, the two can nail 9 nails a minute. After 11 minutes, the two will have nailed 99 nails, and 11 is the best estimate.

6. What is the perimeter of a triangle with vertices (2, –1), (6, –1), and (6, –4)?

A. 7

B. 9

C. 12

D. 14

6. The correct answer is C. First use the points to draw out the triangle you are given. You will find that the triangle looks something like this:

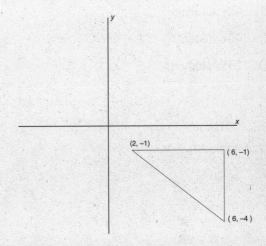

The base of the triangle is 4, and its height is 3. According to the Pythagorean theorem ($a^2 + b^2 = c^2$), the third side is 5 (a 3-4-5 triplet). The perimeter is 3 + 4 + 5 = 12.

7. Clint scored a 94 on his biology test. That was 8 more points than his average on his first four tests. In order to find his combined score on all five tests, which of the following equations can be used to solve the problem?

A. $4x + 94 = 86$

B. $86 + 94 \times 4 = x$

C. $(86 \times 4) + 94 = x$

D. $(94 \times 4) = x - 86$

7. Answer choice C is correct. Your goal is to find the total for five exams. You know one of them, a score of 94. To determine the score of the other four, use your knowledge of averages. There are four tests, which give an average of 86 (8 lower than 94). To find this total, multiply 86 × 4. Combining these two terms will give you the total. C represents this in equation format.

8. At a local high school, x out of every 5 students go to Butterick College. If there are 240 students, how many are expected to go to Butterick College?

A. 12x students

B. 48x students

C. 60x students

D. 235x students

8. The correct answer is B. This is a proportion question. We are told that x students go to Butterick College for every 5 total students. If we set this equal to our unknown relationship, we have the equation:

$$\frac{x \text{ students to Butterick}}{5 \text{ total}} = \frac{\text{total expected to go}}{240 \text{ total}}$$

We can cross multiply to get

$$240x = 5(\text{Expected Number})$$

Divide by 5 to get our answer

$$48x = (\text{Expected Number})$$

9. Right triangle ABC has lengths of 3, 4, and a hypotenuse of x. Right triangle DEF has lengths of x, 12, and a hypotenuse of y. What is the value of x + y?

A. 5

B. 12

C. 13

D. 18

9. The correct answer is D. Use your knowledge of Pythagorean Triplets to find that $x = 5$ (a 3-4-5 right triangle). Next, you can find y by recognizing the 5, 12, 13 right triangle. The sum of $x + y = 5 + 13$, or 18.

10. Kathleen has two coins. What is the probability that, after flipping those coins, she will get one head and one tail?

A. 1

B. $\frac{3}{4}$

C. $\frac{1}{2}$

D. $\frac{1}{4}$

10. Answer choice C is the correct answer. There are two possible outcomes of the four total possibilities:

H   H

H   T

T   T

T   H

11. Find two numbers that have a sum of 58 and a difference of 16:

   A. 5, 21

   B. 16, 42

   C. 21, 37

   D. −16, 74

11. The correct answer is C. To solve the problem, you can either write a series of simultaneous equations, or simply backsolve and plug in the answer choices. If you plug in, you'll notice that answer choice A does not yield a sum of 58. Answer choices C and D do not have a difference of 16. Only C works. If you write two equations, your equations should look like this:

$$x + y = 58$$

$$x - y = 16$$

12. If $x = 5$, find the value of $\dfrac{4x+2}{2x}$.

   A. 4

   B. 5

   C. 2.2

   D. 220

12. The answer is C. First, we need to substitute the value of 5 wherever we see x in the equation.

$$\frac{4 \cdot 5 + 2}{2 \cdot 5}$$

$$= \frac{20 + 2}{10}$$

$$= \frac{22}{10}$$

$$= 2.2$$

13. A rectangle has sides $(3a - 7)$ and $(5a + 4)$. What is the perimeter of the rectangle?

   A. $8a - 3$

   B. $15a - 28$

   C. $6a - 14$

   D. $16a - 6$

13. The correct answer is D. A rectangle has equal lengths and equal widths. To find the perimeter, add: $2(3a - 7) + 2(5a + 4)$ to get:

$$6a - 14 + 10a + 8 =$$

$$16a - 6$$

14. What is the solution to $(x^2 + 2x - 9) + (x - 2)$?

 A. $x^3 + 2x^2 - 11$

 B. $x^2 + 3x - 9x - 11$

 C. $x^2 + 3x - 11$

 D. $x^3 + 2x^2 - 11x$

14. The correct answer is C. Remember that when you're adding, you can only combine like variables (same letter, and to the same power).

15. If $\sqrt{2y - 7} = \sqrt{3 + 4y}$, what is the value of y?

 A. -10

 B. -5

 C. 5

 D. 8

15. The correct answer is B. To solve this, square both sides of the equation. This will give you the following result:

$$2y - 7 = 3 + 4y$$

$$-7 = 3 + 2y$$

$$-10 = 2y$$

$$-5 = y$$

16. What is the range of the equation $y = x^2$?

 A. All real numbers

 B. All negative real numbers

 C. All positive real numbers

 D. All real numbers greater than or equal to 0

16. The correct answer is D. The best way to solve this question to is to try some numbers for the value of x (the range), and see what comes out for the domain (the y value):

If $x = 2$, $y = 4$. So eliminate B.

If $x = 0$, $y = 0$. So eliminate C.

Can you get a negative number? No. x^2 will always be positive — so you can eliminate answer choice A.

17. $\dfrac{4.5 \times 10^7}{9.0 \times 10^3} =$

   A. 5×10^{10}

   B. 5×10^3

   C. 5×10^4

   D. 5×10^{10}

17. The correct answer is B Treat the coefficients and the powers of 10 separately.

$\dfrac{4.5}{9} = .5$ and $\dfrac{10^7}{10^3} = 10^4$. Combine the two: $.5 \times 10^4 = 5 \times 10^3$, and B is the correct answer.

18. A line with slope 2 passes through $(-6, 7)$ and $(2, p)$. What is the value of p?

   A. 2

   B. 11

   C. 14

   D. 23

18. The correct answer is D. Set up the slope equation: $m = \dfrac{rise}{run}$.

$$2 = \dfrac{p-7}{2-(-6)}$$
$$2 = \dfrac{p-7}{8}$$
$$16 = p - 7$$
$$23 = p$$

19. The solution set to $|2x - 4| = 10$ is:

   A. -10 only

   B. -3 only

   C. -10 and -3

   D. -3 and 7

19. The correct answer is D. When solving an equation with an absolute value, you can set up a series of equations, or you could also Backsolve by plugging in the answer choices. The equations are: $2x - 4 = 10$, and $2x - 4 = -10$. The first equation can be solved to get $x = 7$. Now you immediately know that D is correct, because it is the only answer choice that contains 7. The second equation yields $x = -3$.

20. The solution of $|2y - 6| = -9$ is:

A. $-\dfrac{2}{3}, \dfrac{3}{2}$

B. $-\dfrac{3}{2}, \dfrac{15}{2}$

C. $-\dfrac{2}{3}, \dfrac{7}{2}$

D. $-\dfrac{2}{3}, -\dfrac{3}{2}$

20. The correct answer is B. To find the solution with an equation that includes absolute value, set up two equalities:

$$2y - 6 = -9 \quad \text{and} \quad 2y - 6 = 9$$

$$y = -\dfrac{3}{2} \qquad y = \dfrac{15}{2}$$

21. If $9a - 6 = 30 - 3a$, then $a =$

A. 2

B. 3

C. 4

D. 6

21. The correct answer is B. Solve for a by isolating the variable in the equation:

$$12a - 6 = 30$$

$$12a = 36$$

$$a = 3$$

22. Marty keeps a collection of pennies, nickels, and dimes in his desk. If he has twice as many dimes as nickels, three times as many pennies as dimes, and $6x$ worth of pennies, then the value of his pennies, nickels, and dimes in cents equals:

A. $360x$

B. $100x$

C. $31x$

D. x

22. The correct answer is C. You should be able to easily eliminate answer choice D. It is smaller than the amount of pennies you're given. Break up the sentence into pieces in order to solve the problem. You know we have $6x$ pennies, and you know that we have three times as many pennies than dimes, so there are $2x$ dimes. To change this to the value of cents, there are $20x$ cents. Next, if there are $2x$ dimes, then there are x nickels. To translate this into cents, multiply by 5 to get $5x$ cents. In summation, there are $6x + 20x + 5x = 31x$ cents.

23. Solve the following equation for w:

$.83w + .29 = .5w - .7$

A. $-.3$

B. -3

C. -3.3

D. 3.3

23. The correct answer is B. Be very careful to watch your decimal places and positive as well as negative signs. You can either Backsolve to find the correct answer, or manipulate the equation as follows:

$.83w + .29 = .5w - .7$

$.33w = -.99$

$w = -\dfrac{.99}{.33}$ (divide both sides by .33)

$w = -3$

24. A solution of paint that is 100% yellow is to be combined with a solution that is 80% yellow to make 50L of paint that is 84% yellow. How many liters of the 100% yellow solution are needed?

A. 42

B. 40

C. 10

D. 8

24. The correct answer is C. In order to solve this mixture problem, set up a chart like the one below:

	Percent Yellow	Amount of Solution	Amount of Mixture
First Solution	100%	x	x
Second Solution	80%	50-x	40 − .8x
Third Solution	84%	50	(.84)(50)

Set up an equation to give you the following:

$x + 40 - .8x = (.84)(50)$

$.2x + 40 = 42$

$.2x = 2$

$x = 10$

25. Ana is playing a card game. She is holding 5 diamonds and 3 clubs. If she plays two cards at random, what is the probability that she plays two diamonds?

A. $\dfrac{5}{14}$

B. $\dfrac{25}{56}$

C. $\dfrac{9}{14}$

D. $\dfrac{67}{56}$

25. Answer choice A is correct. There are two events in this problem—the first card that she plays, and the second card that she plays. For the first card, there are a total of eight cards, 5 of which are diamonds. The probability of playing a diamond on the first card is $\dfrac{5}{8}$. If this occurs, there are then 7 cards left, 4 of which are diamonds. Thus, the probability of playing a second diamond is $\dfrac{4}{7}$. Multiply to get the combined probability:

$$\left(\frac{5}{8}\right)\left(\frac{4}{7}\right) = \frac{20}{56} = \frac{5}{14}$$

26. Simplify the following expression:

$$\frac{(4a^2b^5)^3}{(2a^1b^0)^2}$$

A. $16a^4b^{15}$

B. $3a^7b^{13}$

C. $16a^7b^{13}$

D. $3a^7b^{15}$

26. A is the correct answer. Simplifying the expression requires you to use the rules for exponents, and follow the order of operations. Process of Elimination can be a helpful tool for these types of questions—but make sure you deal with each variable and coefficient one step at a time. Let's start with the coefficients: $4^3 = 64$; $2^2 = 4$; is 16. We can eliminate B and D. We are now left with answer choices A and C. Look at the variable a. a^2 raised to the third power is a^6 (remember to multiply the exponents).

a^1 squared is a^2, so $\dfrac{a^6}{a^2} = a^4$ (remember to subtract the exponents when dividing).

27. Which of the following (a, b) coordinates is a solution of the system?

$$\{a + b = -1\}$$

$$\{b + 3a = 4\}$$

A. $\left(\dfrac{7}{2}, \dfrac{5}{2}\right)$

B. $\left(\dfrac{7}{2}, -\dfrac{5}{2}\right)$

C. $\left(\dfrac{5}{2}, \dfrac{7}{2}\right)$

D. $\left(\dfrac{5}{2}, -\dfrac{7}{2}\right)$

27. The correct answer is D. Normally, when given a system of two equations, you would need to use the substitution method in order to find the values of x and y. Here, with answer choices available to you, simply plug them in to see which ones work. Only answer choice D gives you the correct answer. If you wanted to solve using substitution (a longer method), you would need to do the following:

$$b + 3a = 4$$

$$(-a - 1) + 3a = 4$$

$$2a - 1 = 4$$

$$2a = 5$$

$$a = \frac{5}{2}$$

$$b + 3\left(\frac{5}{2}\right) = 4$$

$$b + \frac{15}{2} = 4$$

$$b = 4 - \frac{15}{2}$$

$$b = -\frac{7}{2}$$

28. Which of the following lines is parallel to $3x - y = -5$?

    A. $y = 5x - 3$

    B. $y = 4x - 5$

    C. $5y - 15x = 10$

    D. $15y - 5x = 3$

28. The correct answer is C. To determine which line is parallel, first find the slope of the line given. Rearrange the line to put it in the proper slope-intercept form: $y = mx + b$. This makes the line: $y = 3x + 5$, and the slope is 3, so we need to find a line with a slope of 3 in the answer choices. The slope of line A is 5; the slope of line B is 4. The slope of line C is 3, and that is the correct answer.

29. The area of a rectangle is $4a^2 + 14a + 12$. If the length of the rectangle is $(2a + 3)$, what is the value of the width of the rectangle?

    A. $2a + 11$

    B. $a^4 + 8a + 9$

    C. $2a + 3$

    D. $2a + 4$

29. The correct answer is D. Divide the polynomial term by the length of rectangle:

$$2a + 3 \overline{) 4a^2 + 14a + 12}$$

The solution is below:

$$
\begin{array}{r}
2a + 4 \\
2a + 3 \overline{) 4a^2 + 14a + 12} \\
= 4a^2 + 6a \\
= 8a + 12 \\
8a + 12
\end{array}
$$

30. A square has sides $(-3, 0)$, $(1, -3)$, $(4, 1)$ and $(0, k)$. What is the value of k?

    A. 1

    B. 3

    C. 4

    D. 5

30. The correct answer is C. This question is quite difficult, and may take some time. First, plot all the points you know. Because this is a square, all sides must have equal length. You can take look at any two points to find that the length of the side of the square is 5. (You can make a hidden 3-4-5 triangle.). Do this same thing with the missing point to get a value of 4.

ANSWERS AND EXPLANATIONS FOR SESSION TWO

Grid-In Answer Key

1. 18.7
2. 2
3. 20
4. 42
5. Any number between 3 and 8
6. 12
7. 6/55, or .1091
8. 5
9. 8
10. 12

Grid-In Explanations

1. The correct answer is $\frac{56}{3}$ or 18.7. To find this answer, manipulate the equation by isolating the variable, as follows:

$$7y - 2 = 22 + 32 + 4y$$

$$3y = 22 + 32 + 2$$

$$3y = 56$$

$$y = \frac{56}{3}, \text{ or } 18.7$$

You may grid in either $\frac{56}{3}$, or 18.7. If you choose to put the number in decimal form, the number 18.66666 rounds (to the nearest tenth) to 18.7.

2. The correct answer is 2. To find this answer, isolate the variables from the remainder of the equation, as follows:

$$8x - 12y = -12y - 6x + 28$$

$$14x = 28$$

$$x = 2$$

3. The correct answer is 20. To find this solution, use your knowledge of consecutive integers to set up the following equation:

$$x + (x + 1) + (x + 2) + (x + 3) = 86$$

$$4x + 6 = 86$$

$$4x = 80$$

$$x = 20$$

Or you could look at the numbers and realize that the consecutive numbers have to be around 20. If you start with 20 as the lowest number you've hit on the answer without doing any calculations!

4. The correct answer is 42. Be careful not to do too much work here. From the first equation, you can find that $x^2 = 35$. There is no need to calculate the square root of this value—the qw'''tion asks for you for the value of $x^2 + 7$. So, if x^2 is 35, then the solution is 35 + 7, or 42.

5. There are several correct answer to this problem, all of which are expressed by:

$$3 < x + y < 8$$

Any number between 3 and 8 that will fit in the grid will work. Because x and y need not be integers, you can use decimals if you choose. The easiest thing to do is to pick a value for x, pick a value for y, and add them together. For example:

$$x = 2 \qquad y = 4.5$$

$$x + y = 6.5$$

6. The correct answer is 12. To find this answer, factor the original equation:

$$2y^2 + 5y - k = (y + 4)(\,?\,)$$

$$= (y + 4)(2y - ?)$$

$$= (y + 4)(2y - 3)$$

We know that the second term includes $2y$ (to get us to $2y^2$), and will contain a minus sign (the term k is negative). The number must be 3 in order to get us to $5y$. Therefore, $k = 12$.

7. The correct answer is $\frac{6}{55}$, or .1091 in decimal form. The probability of his drawing the first red marble is $\frac{4}{11}$. (There are four "red" outcomes out of a total of 11 possible outcomes.) Next, the probability of selecting another red marble is $\frac{3}{10}$. (There are three outcomes, out of a total of 10 possible outcomes.) Note that the marbles selected are not replaced. Thus, the probability is $\frac{4}{11} \times \frac{3}{10} = \frac{12}{110} = \frac{6}{55}$

8. You could think of what factors of 24 have only one number between them. The most likely pair is 6 and 4, and 5 is the number between them—it's your answer. Alternately, you could set up an algebraic equation, which would look like this: $(x + 1)(x - 1) = 24$. To solve this equation, you could try a few numbers, or multiply the equation to get:

$$x^2 - 1 = 24$$

$$x^2 = 25$$

$$x = 5$$

9. The correct answer is 8. First, find the slope of the line, using the difference of two points $m = \dfrac{\text{rise}}{\text{run}}$:

$$slope = \frac{6 - 3}{6 - 5} = \frac{3}{1} = 3$$

With a slope of 3, we can now find y by setting up the equation again:

$$3 = \frac{12 - 6}{y - 6}$$
$$3 = \frac{6}{y - 6}$$
$$3y - 18 = 6$$
$$3y = 24$$
$$y = 8$$

10. To find the value of y, first make all the denominators the same (find a common denominator).

$$\frac{12(7)}{12(y)} - \frac{4y(1)}{4y(3)} = \frac{3y(1)}{3y(4)}$$

So now they all have the denominator $12y$, and you can solve, disregarding the denominator.

$$84 - 4y = 3y$$

$$84 = 7y$$

$$y = 12$$

Written Response Explanation

1. *Completing the square* is a technique used to solve quadratic equations. The first step in this process is to put the equation in the following form:

$$2x^2 + 3x = 3$$

$$x^2 + \frac{3}{2}x = \frac{3}{2}$$

Next, we need to complete the square by dividing the number next to x by 2:

$$\left(\frac{3}{2}\right)\left(\frac{1}{2}\right) = \left(\frac{3}{4}\right)$$

Thus, you need to add $\left(\frac{3}{4}\right) \times \left(\frac{3}{4}\right)$ in order to complete the square:

$$x^2 + \frac{3}{2}x + \frac{9}{16} = \frac{3}{2} + \frac{9}{16}$$

$$\left(x + \frac{3}{4}\right)\left(x + \frac{3}{4}\right) = \frac{24}{16} + \frac{9}{16}$$

$$\left(x + \frac{3}{4}\right)^2 = \frac{33}{16}$$

$$x = \frac{3}{4} + \frac{\sqrt{33}}{4} \text{ and } \frac{3}{4} - \frac{\sqrt{33}}{4}$$

In order to get full credit for part I, you will need to come up with these values for x. Further, you will need to show that you got these values by completing the square (and not by the quadratic formula!).

2 & 3. The discriminant is the term under the square root in the quadratic formula; $b^2 - 4ac$. It can be used to determine how many real-number solutions exist to a quadratic equation. In order to find the value of the discriminant, we need to set up the quadratic equation in standard form:

$$2x^2 + 3x - 3 = 0$$

$$a = 2, b = 3, c = -3$$

(This, if labeled clearly, will also give you the solution to part 3.)

Now, with this information, the discriminant equals:

$$(3)^2 - 4(2)(-3) =$$

$$9 - (-24) = 33$$

The value 33, because it is a positive number, will tell you that there are two real number solutions to this equation. While you already know this from step 1, you still have to show your work to get the points.

4.

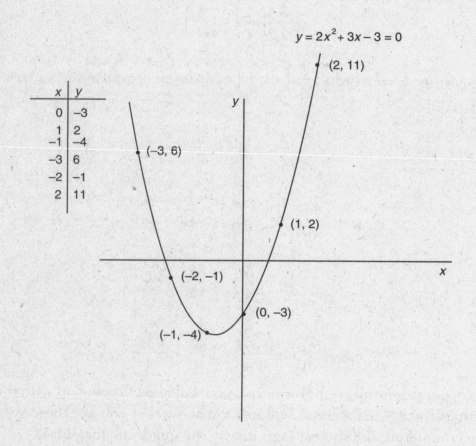

Make sure your graph is clearly labeled. If you have a graphing calculator, you can get a feel for what the equation should look like. Regardless, plug in easy values until you get a complete picture for the graph. It does not need to be a perfect graph—just make sure everything is clearly labeled.

ABOUT THE AUTHOR

Rick Sliter joined The Princeton Review in 1994 after graduating with a degree in Quantitative Economics and Decision Sciences at the University of California, San Diego. Rick worked in two California offices, recently serving as Executive Director of The Princeton Review in Palo Alto.

Nationally, Rick has served on research and development teams to produce course materials for the SAT-I, SAT-II, and GMAT. This is his second series of books published by The Princeton Review. In 1998, he wrote *Cracking the CBEST*, a guide to help aspiring teachers in California pass the CBEST exam.

Rick currently lives in Los Angeles, pursuing a MBA at the Anderson School at UCLA.

NOTES

NOTES

NOTES

NOTES

NOTES

NOTES

NOTES

NOTES

www.review.com

Expert Advice

Counselor-O-Matic

Pop Surveys

www.review.com

Paying for It

www.review.com

THE PRINCETON REVIEW

Getting In

Word du Jour

www.review.com

www.review.com

College Talk

Find-O-Rama College Search

www.review.com

Best Schools

SAT Survival

We have a smarter way to get better grades in school.

Find a tutor in 3 easy steps:

Find.
Log onto our website: **www.tutor.com**

Connect.
Sign up to find a tutor who fits all your needs

Learn.
Get **tutored** in any subject or skill

Visit www.tutor.com

MORE EXPERT ADVICE
ON ALL YOUR IMPORTANT EXAMS

THE PRINCETON REVIEW

CRACKING THE SAT & PSAT
2000 EDITION
0-375-75403-2 • $18.00

CRACKING THE SAT & PSAT WITH
SAMPLE TESTS ON CD-ROM
2000 EDITION
0-375-75404-0 • $29.95

SAT MATH WORKOUT
0-679-75363-X • $15.00

SAT VERBAL WORKOUT
0-679-75362-1 • $16.00

CRACKING THE ACT
2000-2001 EDITION
0-375-75500-4 • $18.00

CRACKING THE ACT WITH
SAMPLE TESTS ON CD-ROM
2000-2001 EDITION
0-375-75501-2 • $29.95

CRASH COURSE FOR THE ACT
10 Easy Steps to Higher Score
0-375-75326-5 • $9.95

CRASH COURSE FOR THE SAT
10 Easy Steps to Higher Score
0-375-75324-9 • $9.95

CRACKING THE CLEP 4TH EDITION
0-375-76151-9 • $20.00

CRACKING THE GOLDEN STATE EXAMS:
1ST YEAR ALGEBRA
0-375-75352-4 • $16.00

CRACKING THE GOLDEN STATE EXAMS:
BIOLOGY
0-375-75356-7 • $16.00

CRACKING THE GOLDEN STATE EXAMS:
CHEMISTRY
0-375-75357-5 • $16.00

CRACKING THE GOLDEN STATE EXAMS:
ECONOMICS
0-375-75355-9 • $16.00

CRACKING THE GOLDEN STATE EXAMS:
GEOMETRY
0-375-75353-2 • $16.00

CRACKING THE GOLDEN STATE EXAMS:
U.S. HISTORY
0-375-75354-0 • $16.00

WE ALSO HAVE BOOKS TO HELP YOU SCORE HIGH ON

THE SAT II AND AP EXAMS:

CRACKING THE AP BIOLOGY EXAM 2000-2001 EDITION
0-375-75495-4 • $17.00

CRACKING THE AP CALCULUS EXAM AB & BC 2000-2001 EDITION
0-375-75499-7 • $18.00

CRACKING THE AP CHEMISTRY EXAM 2000-2001 EDITION
0-375-75497-0 • $17.00

CRACKING THE AP ECONOMICS EXAM (MACRO & MICRO) 2000-2001 EDITION
0-375-75507-1 • $17.00

CRACKING THE AP ENGLISH LITERATURE EXAM 2000-2001 EDITION
0-375-75493-8 • $17.00

CRACKING THE AP U.S. GOVERNMENT AND POLITICS EXAM 2000-2001 EDITION
0-375-75496-2 • $17.00

CRACKING THE AP U.S. HISTORY EXAM 2000-2001 EDITION
0-375-75494-6 • $17.00

CRACKING THE AP PHYSICS 2000-2001 EDITION
0-375-75492-X • $19.00

CRACKING THE AP PSYCHOLOGY 2000-2001 EDITION
0-375-75480-6 • $17.00

CRACKING THE AP EUROPEAN HISTORY 2000-2001 EDITION
0-375-75498-9 • $17.00

CRACKING THE AP SPANISH 2000-2001 EDITION
0-75401-4 • $17.00

CRACKING THE SAT II: BIOLOGY SUBJECT TEST 1999-2000 EDITION
0-375-75297-8 • $17.00

CRACKING THE SAT II: CHEMISTRY SUBJECT TEST 1999-2000 EDITION
0-375-75298-6 • $17.00

CRACKING THE SAT II: ENGLISH SUBJECT TEST 1999-2000 EDITION
0-375-75295-1 • $17.00

CRACKING THE SAT II: FRENCH SUBJECT TEST 1999-2000 EDITION
0-375-75299-4 • $17.00

CRACKING THE SAT II: HISTORY SUBJECT TEST 1999-2000 EDITION
0-375-75300-1 • $17.00

CRACKING THE SAT II: MATH SUBJECT TEST 1999-2000 EDITION
0-375-75296-X • $17.00

CRACKING THE SAT II: PHYSICS SUBJECT TEST 1999-2000 EDITION
0-375-75302-8 • $17.00

CRACKING THE SAT II: SPANISH SUBJECT TEST 1999-2000 EDITION
0-375-75301-X • $17.00

Visit Your Local Bookstore or Order Direct by Calling 1-800-733-3000
www.randomhouse.com/princetonreview

FIND US...

International

Hong Kong
4/F Sun Hung Kai Centre
30 Harbour Road, Wan Chai,
Hong Kong
Tel: (011)85-2-517-3016

Japan
Fuji Building 40, 15-14
Sakuragaokacho, Shibuya Ku,
Tokyo 150, Japan
Tel: (011)81-3-3463-1343

Korea
Tae Young Bldg, 944-24,
Daechi- Dong, Kangnam-Ku
The Princeton Review—ANC
Seoul, Korea 135-280,
South Korea
Tel: (011)82-2-554-7763

Mexico City
PR Mex S De RL De Cv
Guanajuato 228 Col. Roma
06700 Mexico D.F., Mexico
Tel: 525-564-9468

Montreal
666 Sherbrooke St.
West, Suite 202
Montreal, QC H3A 1E7 Canada
Tel: 514-499-0870

Pakistan
1 Bawa Park - 90 Upper Mall
Lahore, Pakistan
Tel: (011)92-42-571-2315

Spain
Pza. Castilla, 3 - 5º A, 28046
Madrid, Spain
Tel: (011)341-323-4212

Taiwan
155 Chung Hsiao East Road
Section 4 - 4th Floor,
Taipei R.O.C., Taiwan
Tel: (011)886-2-751-1243

Thailand
Building One, 99 Wireless Road
Bangkok, Thailand 10330
Tel: 662-256-7080

Toronto
1240 Bay Street, Suite 300
Toronto M5R 2A7 Canada
Tel: 800-495-7737
Tel: 716-839-4391

Vancouver
4212 University Way NE,
Suite 204
Seattle, WA 98105
Tel: 206-548-1100

National (U.S.)

We have more than 60 offices around the U.S. and run courses at over 400 sites. For courses and locations within the U.S. call 1-800-2-Review and you will be routed to the nearest office.

4326